DRIFTERS

To Charlie
In solidarity for
the love of our
oceans
Pam Longobardi

PAM LONGOBARDI

∞

DRIFTERS

∞

Plastics, Pollution, and Personhood

CHARTA

Design
Mario Piazza, Letizia Abbate (46xy studio)

Editorial Coordination
Filomena Moscatelli

Copyediting
Emily Ligniti

Copywriting and Press Office
Silvia Palombi

US Editorial Director
Francesca Sorace

Promotion and Web
Monica D'Emidio

Distribution
Antonia De Besi

Administration
Grazia De Giosa

Warehouse and Outlet
Roberto Curiale

ISBN 978-88-8158-770-4

Printed in Italy

Cover
Eye of the Ocean, 2009 (detail)
defunct and devalued currency, ink, glass beads and pinpricks on paper, 24 x 20 in.

Photo Credits
Saatchi & Saatchi LA for Surfrider Foundation, p. 18
Claire Johnson Fackler and NOAA Office of National Marine Sanctuary, p. 21
David Rothstein, p. 22
Mark Dion and In Situ Fabienne Leclerc Gallery, Paris p. 25
All remaining photos by Pam Longobardi

Edizioni Charta srl
Milano
via della Moscova, 27 - 20121
Tel. +39-026598098/026598200
Fax +39-026598577
e-mail: charta@chartaartbooks.it

Charta Books Ltd.
New York City
Tribeca Office
Tel. +1-313-406-8468
e-mail: international@chartaartbooks.it

www.chartaartbooks.it

ACKNOWLEDGEMENTS

As with all things that are a culmination over time of a series of events, energies, serendipities, and pure faith, it will be impossible to list all the contributing persons whose large or small actions created the ripple effect that lead to the shores of this book. My list will be incomplete, but you know who you are. With that said, I start here:

I thank those individuals, institutions, and collectives that have exhibited or supported this project from the beginning: Robin Sandler and Debbie Hudson of Sandler Hudson Gallery, Atlanta; Victor Faccinto of Wake Forest University; Peggy Cyphers and the visionary Broadthinking Curatorial Project; Jeanne Voltura and the City of Las Vegas Cultural Program; Susan Tinney of Tinney Contemporary, Nashville; Abraham Lubelski of NY ARTS Beijing; Martha Kjeseth Johnson at the Maier Museum; Marthe Keller and Paola Iacucci of the BAU Institute; Simonetta Gorreri of Artlife in Venice, and Olger Rojas Elizondo of UNA Nicoya, Costa Rica. And to Georgia State University for its support of my research.

I thank Francesca Sorace and Giuseppe Liverani of Charta for believing my project needed to be seen by the wider audience made possible by this book; Carl Safina, Dores Sacquegna, Ron Broglio, and Suzi Gablik for their powerful and thoughtful words gracing its pages; and Mark Dion and Saatchi and Saatchi for the loan of their images. And I thank elin o'Hara slavick for introducing me to Francesca and Giuseppe in the first place, and to Margery Amdur for introducing us all through her amazing symposium.

I thank my tactical collaborators/philosophical allies David Rothstein in Hawai'i and Andrea Verardo in Venice for their logistical assistance, support, and friendship. I thank Chris Pair for his technical expertise with the film and the website. I also thank Captain Charlie Moore and the Algalita Marine Research Foundation, and Kris McElwee and Carey Morishige of the NOAA Marine Debris Program, for their help and their work to educate us all. And I thank Wayne Sentman of Oceanic Society for all present and future collaboration efforts, and Cynthia Vanderlip for introducing us and for the tireless work she does on behalf of the creatures of Kure Atolland, the Papahanaumokuakea National Marine Monument.

I thank Craig Dongoski, Brianna and Gretel, and my family for their love and support everyday, and for forgiving me when I have to be away.

Finally, I thank all those people who actively love and care for the earth and its life forms, and everyone who tends the world beaches by picking up trash (that doesn't belong there) instead of shells (that do).

FOREWORD

Carl Safina

Encircled by water to the round horizon, a sleek albatross on 7 foot wings glides in for a landing on a lonely atoll in the heart of the ocean. For days, she has flown continually to get here. Her feet have not touched anything solid, nor have her legs supported her weight, for perhaps two weeks, possibly as much as four. She surveys the scene through her lovely, dark, pastel-shadowed eyes, then she calls, "Eh Eh Eh," sounding like a rusty gate.

A hungry chick immediately comes to her. All the chicks are hungry. The adult knows it's not her own chick's voice, and waddles by. One by one, five more chicks come begging and calling as she continues walking. One by one, she gives them a jab with her hooked bill. She walks towards where one particular chick has just started calling. And at that call, she is responding, calling softly, matter-of-factly, with little excitement. She simply walks directly to the chick.

Since the last time she was here, she has traveled perhaps five thousand, maybe ten thousand miles for the meal she will deliver. This is not hypothetical. Researchers were shocked when satellites first revealed these distances. But as the albatrosses have long known, this is merely their routine. I've been there, and I actually saw what follows: parent and youngster meet and greet, the adult knowing that this is her child. People are often amazed that seabirds can recognize each other among thousands. But give them a little credit. We recognize voices on the telephone. We can recognize each other in cities among millions. They, too, can recognize voices and find each other in a crowd. They know what they're doing.

The whining chick begins eagerly nibbling the adult's bill. The adult hunches forward. The chick, with sudden frenzied expectation, thrusts its bill up tight to the adult's gaping mouth, forcing her bill wider and wider.

The adult abruptly pumps out several thick chunks semi-liquefied squid and purplish fish eggs. The chick bolts them down. Both pause. Then the chick presses for more. The adult again arches her neck. But nothing comes. She tries repeatedly.

I wonder if something is wrong.

Slowly, the tip—just the tip—of a green plastic toothbrush emerges in the bird's throat. The sight so unreal, that my mind is asking over and over: are you *sure* that's a *toothbrush*? The chick, in a flurry of furious hunger, demands to be fed.

With her neck arched, the mother cannot pass the straight toothbrush. She re-swallows it and several times repeats the attempt to cough it up. Each time, she fails to get it fully out. Seeing this bird in distress, this vital mother-child interaction interrupted, is very hard to watch. The parent albatross reswallows a final time, and with the toothbrush stuck inside her, wanders away from her chick.

The main message from the albatross is this: no place, no creature, remains apart from you and me—anywhere in the whole world. Seeing a parent albatross gagging up a toothbrush made me realize humanity has no borders. Probably every albatross in the Pacific Ocean has ingested plastic. Where they nest, you see many dead chicks whose rib cages are full of colorful plastic bits and cigarette lighters. We've woven the albatross and many other creatures into our throwaway culture.

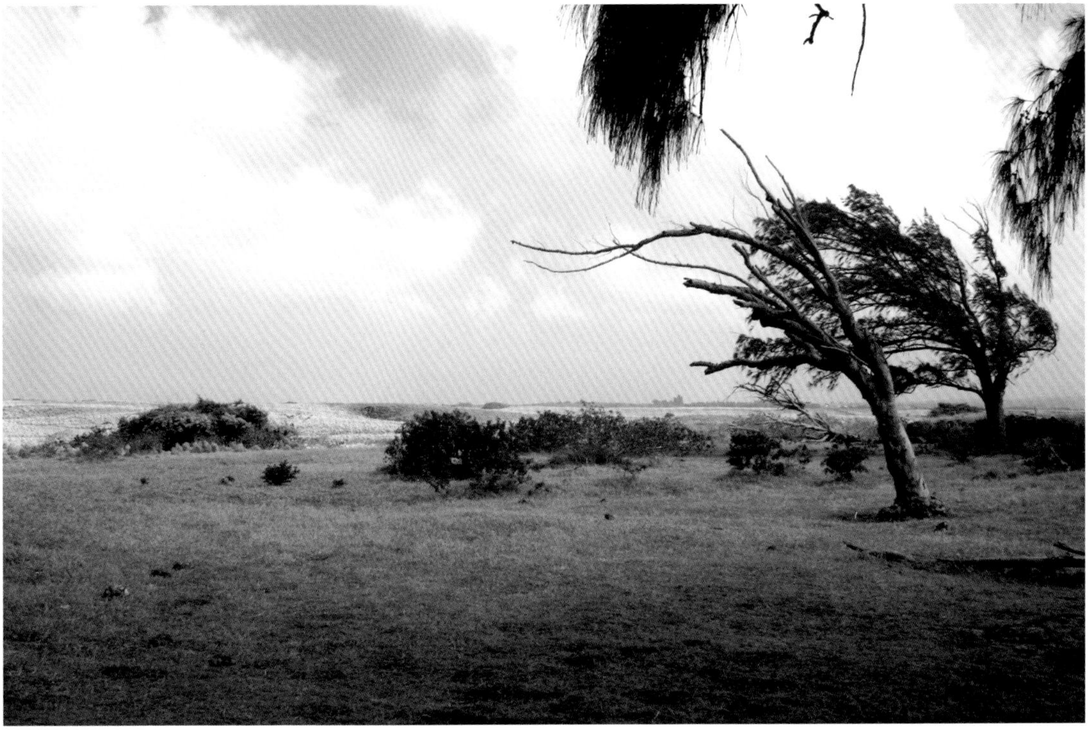

Field with Bougainvillea, 2008, portrait of South Point, digital photograph.

That creates an obligation and the opportunity to make a better world. We need to do this not just for albatrosses, but also for ourselves.

The albatross speaks to us of how much the world is changing, but also how similar we are. As mother albatrosses deliver toothbrushes and cigarette lighters found floating in what has become the plastic soup of the central ocean, human mothers pass toxic chemicals they've absorbed from food and water to their own babies in their milk.

Hundreds of miles from land I have seen sea turtles and sailfish fatally tangled in lost drifting nets. I have seen the most remote oceanic island reefs and beaches loaded with washed-up trash that posed a danger to the wild inhabitants. But we are *all* caught in the same net of life and the same moment in history we are weaving.

Not only is no person an island, no *island* is an island. Albatrosses inhabit only a few islands. Humans inhabit only one, a blue and white marble enclosed in a soap bubble, afloat the great dark sea of space. On that marble, we are all connected, all together.

It's not that *nothing* is being done. People are working to recycle plastic and to clean some of these remote places. But the problem remains much larger than the effort to grapple with it. Many more people need to know, and need to heal the thoughtlessness that is this problem's source. The source isn't just ships; it's anyone's trash that finds its way into a river or waterway.

Gravity creates the illusion that our trash "goes away." Pam Longobardi creates a more realistic illusion: that our trash is a problem we need to confront and conquer. Her work is no mere attempt at creating pretty decoration from found objects. Her work is witness, and in it we share. She gives us a wakeup call, a call to action, a call for change. Her work is art. And the work that art must do is to steer our attention into the path of the oncoming truth. As you're about to see.

BETWEEN MEMORY OF THE PAST AND CHRONICLE OF THE PRESENT

Dores Sacquegna

By now, you may have heard of the floating landfill called the "Pacific Trash Vortex"[1] that travels around the oceans, starting at 500 nautical miles off the coast of California through the South Pacific, Hawai'i, and beyond the reaches almost to Japan. A gigantic mass of plastic, not only of bags and bottles, but also small pieces of polycarbonate particles resembling zooplankton which trick shellfish and fish and end up in the food chain. From this floating plastic soup, Pam Longobardi begins a process of investigation.
In Hawai'i, studying the environment, she finds a landscape different from the ecological paradise so loved by tourists. In front of her eyes, stretches of colored filaments, strings, objects, plastic, various materials dragged by the waves and dumped on the beach among the lava and algae are the sequels of obsessive consumerism of our society, wreckage that the sea brings in its vertiginous tides. They are the consequences of the obsessing consumerism of our society, "property left at death" at the sea's door and transported by its breathtaking tides.

The Memory of Water

Water is memory. To speak about memory is to speak about time, and through internal processing, Longobardi identifies narrative time, the time of a passage, of pauses. Water brings with it the memory of the world, of life that flows slowly, of life that needs dreams and imagination, not the life that aspires to perfection, but that shuns it. The memory of water, the birth of all things transforming themselves, becomes thought and thought disturbance, in order to return to the exact point of departure and to begin another journey there. Harmony and instinct, the instinct that becomes law, the secret of life. In ancient literature, water is the territory of reckless challenge: of overcoming limits in Homer's *Odyssey* and of eternal damnation in the Dantesque hell of the *Divine Comedy*.
Religions and ancient philosophies considered it a source of life and symbol of fertility, renewal and purification, of divine benevolence. Greek philosophy associated the origin of all things with water and explained its flow as the passage of time and change. In China, water was identified with the chaos that gave rise to the universe. Unfortunately, today, man has lost the memory of the sacredness of associating time to water, which inspired respect for this element and its importance to life.
Pam Longobardi's research springs from the problem of waste that pollutes the sea and beaches. In her works we are confronted with a kind of organic architecture, capable of promoting a new harmony between man and nature. Pam Longobardi, calling between environmentalism and the study of natural sciences, invites us to reflect and consider how the contemporary culture of consumerism, fashion, the New Economy, and globalization have become the mythology of the future. Our "contemporary" is the process of cosmogony that does not think of history but of status symbols in a varied inventory of mass that is losing the sense of norms, values, and concepts.
From the hybridization of forms to the transformation of materials, Longobardi transports us into a kind of "Wonderland" where she, like Alice, moves in a dimension of simultaneous events, feelings, and images that somehow restores the idea of a world in which everything

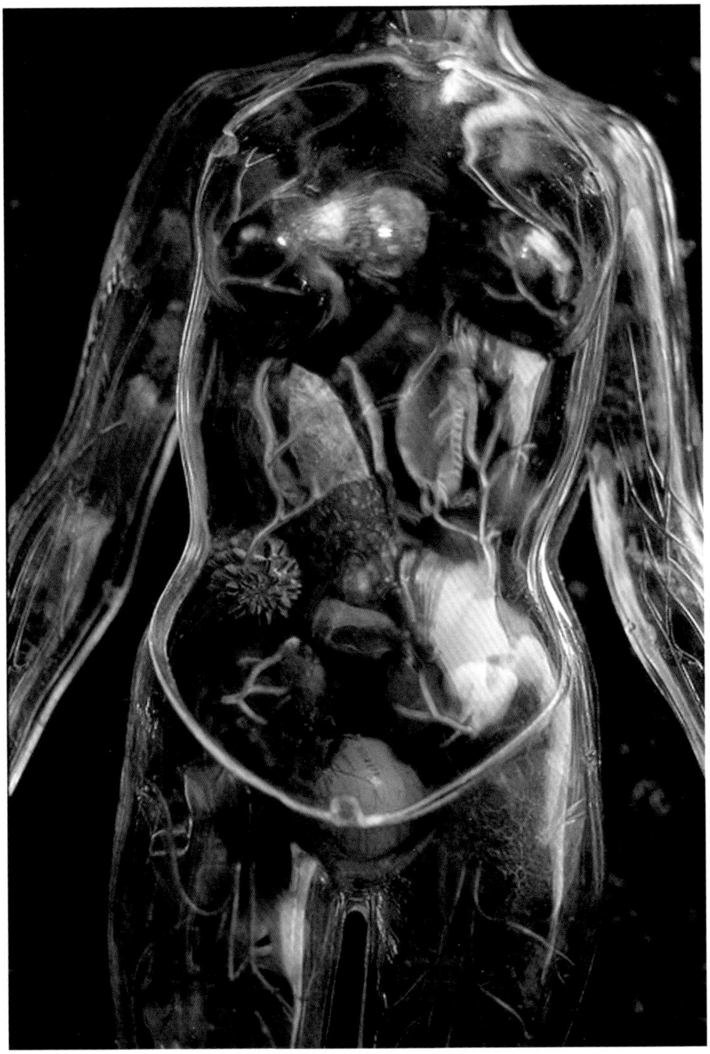

Full, 1991, color cibachrome print, 20 x 16 in.

has a potential impact on everything else, where the figure of this hybrid material recalls the hybridization of cultures, the encounter between different traditions, the product of a continuous stream that has roots in a local context, but that is evolving as a process of interchange between culture, territory, and identity,[2] a network of broadcasting information, transition, and interaction with the world.

Panthalassa

Longobardi chose this name in memory of an ocean, when Pangaea was a continent. To Panthalassa, the artist has dedicated a series of works on display in a recent solo exhibition in Venice.[3] The choice of venue was no accident. Venice is a city on the sea, crossed by narrow streets and bridges linking the mainland to the lagoon. This ancient city, mindful of a past of great splendor and cultural rigor, is today a metaphor for the decay of humanity; the ancient palaces of the "Serenissima" (the adjective assigned at the time of the Republic of Venice during the ninth century) are reflected in a lagoon now

polluted by the oil of boats and the waste of consumerism. At Artlife Gallery in Venice, Longobardi presented *Driftweb*, a sort of multi-colored spider web, constructed from an assemblage of nets, rope, and other materials collected from the beaches of Hawai'i, a web reflected in the water that synthesizes the environmental issues with a freedom from the physical condition, projecting us into a dimension of dreaming.
The materials the artist collects come from the world. There doesn't exist a special place from which she draws the soil for her fantasy. On a recent stay in Otranto, a beautiful town in Southern Italy, in one of the fortified rooms of the walled medieval Aragonese castle during an artist residency sponsored by the Bau Institute in New York, the artist created a sculpture entitled *Shipwreck (Unintended Consequences)* with materials collected on the shores of Otranto and other objects mindful of her previous trips. This work was also exhibited in Venice. The installation represents a kind of ghost ship that carries with it a never-ending story and recalls the garbage barge of New York. The artist patiently recovered various materials (wheels, shoes, old toys, plastic parts, tools), assembling them side by side like a puzzle, and reconstructed the ship, the symbol and memory of our time. Longobardi, with sensitivity, transformed this "property left at death" into a kind of organic architecture, capable of promoting new harmony between man and nature by reconstructing a balance between the natural and built environment.

Bodies that Came from the Sea

Bodies Glocal

Delicate and poetic is the series of *Drifter Objects,* which I have synthesized through four thematic cycles: *Bodies Glocal, Bodies to Lose, Bodies-Track,* and *Bodies Poetic.*
The term "glocalization" was born in the 1980s in Japan and then was imported into English sociologic language by Roland Robertson and developed a decade later by Polish sociologist Zygmunt Bauman. This terminology provides a series of relationships between global environment and local context. Glocalization is a set of systems, groups, organizations, and communities that reside in a territory at the center of the question of individual vs. communal boundaries and the physical assets of the person via the group. Specifically, in the works of Pam Longobardi, *Bodies Glocal* are the "desire body," those elements of our contemporary society produced by the great breeding ground that is global capitalism, and that are the bridge to understanding the dynamics of the new post-modern narcissism divided between local and global identity. In the sea, everything moves: from the past (sculptures, pottery fragments, wreckage) to the future (toys, dishwashers, washing machines, televisions, mobile phones): undisputed symbols of the mythology of contemporary *vanitas,* non-biodegradable and very often toxic. The artist gathers the remains of objects that were once loved, desired, possessed, used, and presents their morphological characteristics as aseptic and rarefied.
From the first step of collection follows the selection, cleaning, and "regeneration" into metaphorical language: characterized by the associations created through the photographic documentation of the fragments as "portraits," mixing synonyms and antonyms, de-contextualizing quotidian materials to extend the meaning of everyday life in order to seek stories about the human condition and its fragility (see the works: *brokenletters, milanosole, tinydove, jawscup*). These objects have lost their original shape, function, and membership because they are coated with a glossy patina, revealing evocations of earthly transience.

Bodies to Lose

With bodies to lose, I think of the physicality of the body as mortality. I imagine the artist selecting the most significant objects, the bodies-masked or bodies-fetishized, always poised between being and nonbeing, between perfection and ruin, between origin and mutation (see *blueleg, plasticjaw, winkface, blue armyman, smilemouth, bodyguy, pinkblob, smallbrain*). These objects represent our physical mortality: soldiers, bits of legs, brains. Research on humans as a human being, freed prisoner and executioner, mysterious and mystical, in a mechanism that reveals the double game of life. In these works, the artist appropriates the classic iconography of death, the body abandoned in the place where it all began, the place of myth and combat, the home of Neptune and the mythical Atlantis. These are relics of the industrial age, a bondage between the vegetal world and industry, between the animal and mineral kingdom, [4] a subject imperfect and fragile, free of meanings and rules. The artist picks them up on the beaches and photographs them individually; annulled in an unsettling white background and with this candor, they take on another form, another meaning, becoming almost astral and covered with new light.

Bodies-Track, Retaining the Memory of What They Once Were

In the ancient world, all objects and sculptures were linked to the cults of veneration: astrology for the interpretation of the cosmos and the stars, idols for protection and divination of the horoscope, or chiromancy for knowledge of the guidance of the oracle. Suspended between mythology and history, these discoveries have told us human history, an ancient history of scriptures filled with characters and alphabets, rituals, costumes, secrets, and symbols of the peoples to which they belonged. [5]

For us contemporaries, to discover these evidences means a dip in the past, evoking legends and myths shared by a specific people, imagining these objects have come from far-flung areas battered by the cold winds of the Arctic, or from legendary Thule or the mythical Atlantis. Items that belonged to a community that believed in the power of heaven and earth, air and fire, believed in assays interrogating the stars to understand the seasons and the success of the harvest, the home and the war, life and death. Civilizations that recognized an authentic and civil relationship with nature.

And again, civilization linked to the cult of the "Great Mother" [6]: a woman or goddess who represented the magical authority of the feminine, of wisdom and heightened spirituality as opposed to the duplicitous nature of the "mother." At once loving, protective, and tolerant, or terrible and vindictive. Creation and destruction. And in the middle, men, with their small, grand lives that celebrated the forces of Nature, erecting temples for the god cults. It's not by accident that the pagan gods should dwell on mountaintops or in the depths of the seas; they were the universal archetypes that governed the world of Antiquity.

Longobardi finds contemporary flotsam and jetsam that bespeak the ancient, formed by the sea from all manner of plastic product fragments (see *mayanbead, fishbottle, dragoncastle, flowerballs*).

Finished with the mythical time of gods and heroes, the contemporary world has taken on as its mythical material the veneration of products for their beauty, functionality, and convenience, of ease, speed, and perfection. Modern humanity no longer asks for help from the forces of nature or gods. There is no more Aeolus, the god of winds, to fan the hottest nights of summer, but an air conditioner, small sized and high powered. Today, products are our gods, facilitating our life in all its aspects. [7]

The major brands are fighting to advertise their products on a global stage, to enhance their quality and performance, to certify, label, and invent new ways of relating to the environment. They are not gods but icons of our times, emptied of spiritual significance. Even architecture has changed our way of life. The countryside has been reduced to walled gardens between one building and another, the heavens are now the realm of aircraft, the land, that of cars, and so on.

The sea embraces everything and keeps within its abyssal depths the past and future, antiquities and household appliances, so poetically bound together in a single embrace, leaving to posterity the power to choose what is good and what is bad for the environment and thus to humanity itself. God invites us to recognize the divine within us, to understand

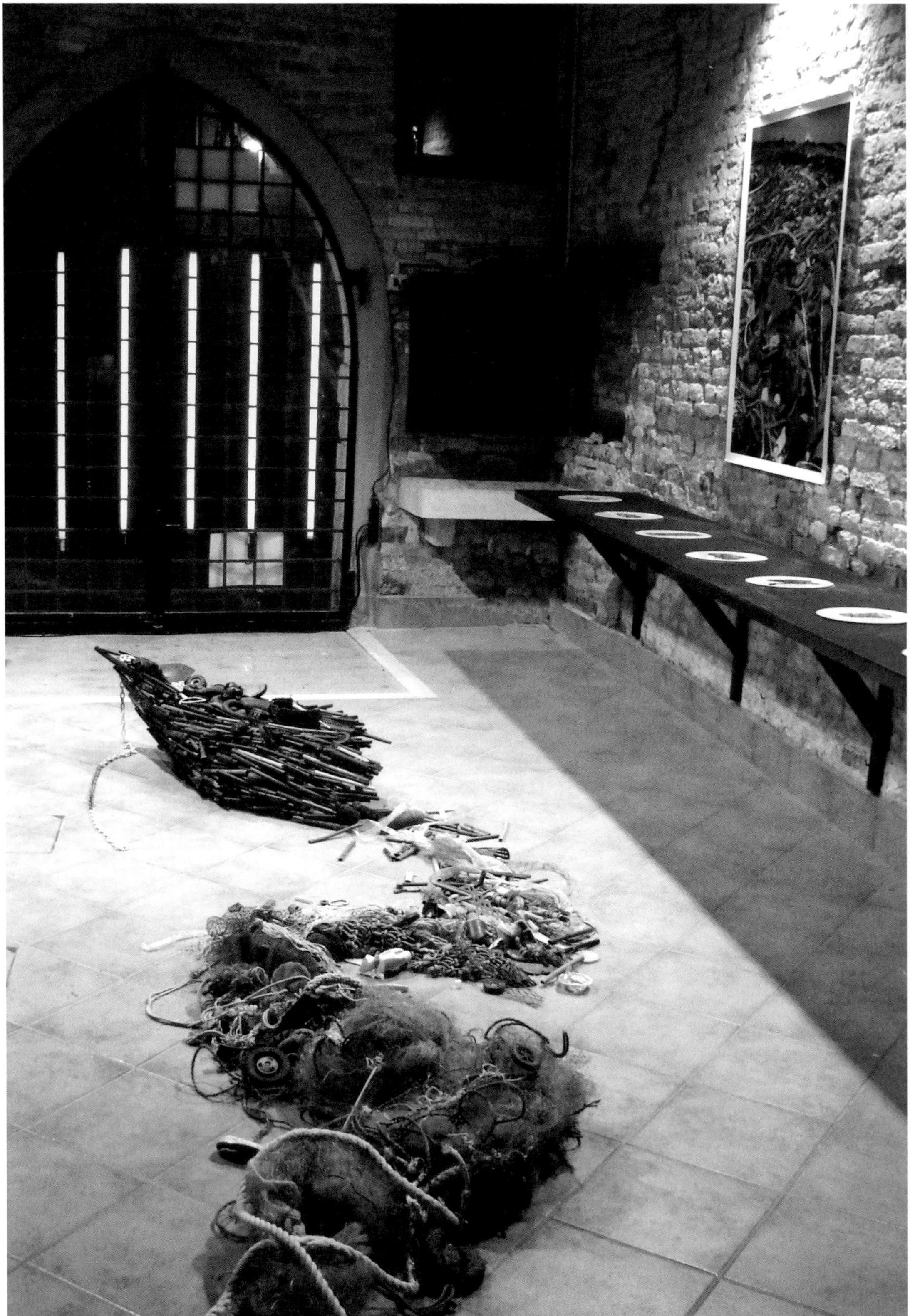

Panthalassa exhibition, 2009, ARTLIFE Gallery, Venice, Italy.

that we are part of the universe and the forces that make it up, creating our image, the image of the world, seeing our own face, the face of our brothers and sisters, and through supreme love to share our essence with the rocks, water, wind, fire, plants, and animals.

Bodies Poetic

The bodies poetic are the narrative bodies, body-objects decontextualized and re-composed in a larger tableau (see *Eye Test Chart: Color Blindness (deadCredC), Defective Flow Chart, Use Value vs Exchange Value*). Like Penelope weaving her web, Longobardi recycles, metaphorically, past and present, setting in motion a mechanism of citations and references, in an increasingly intense emotional tenor. In *Eye Test Chart,* ordering these items side by side, she creates a great mandala, composed of an extraordinary mosaic of plastic shards, plastic bottles, combs, shoes, jewelry, wheels, fishing nets, brushes, screws, pens, toys, positioned in a circle and carefully calibrated in the arrangement of colors. Within her works alternates personal time and narrative time, feelings and memories, myth and reality, water and matter. The motif of the circle recalls the Ouroboros, [8] the serpent-dragon that turns on itself, biting its tail, which defines the evolutionary cycle of life, the archetypal, consisting of thousands of forms, images, symbols, and concepts that combine with each other and contribute to the creation of myth. As we look from the outside, we feel the sensation of crossing into a secret territory, a private place, a tunnel of sensations back in time and from far off, a dim light reveals a disarming poetic corpus that enhances the beauty of its representation. There, among the shapes smoothed by the water, between small combs that have stroked the hair of beautiful girls, between vases where the god Bacchus has quenched their thirst, revives the old myth of a primitive root connected to fertility, femininity, and creation.
Finally, in the installations of Pam Longobardi, past and future, real and tragic dimensions coincide and are interchanged. The objects collected by Longobardi are the product of *mestizo* or "between" cultures, the interactions of different interpretative codes both Western and Eastern. Products that do not remain in a state of crystallization or stagnation are re-assembled by the artist into new forms indigenous to specific identity, a new global identity representing a "locus/place" where they can be identified, recognized, and reflected on.

1. www.inerba.org/Salute-e-Ambiente/Pacific-Trash-Vortex-|-Cinque-milioni-di-chilometri-quadrati-di-rifiuti-nell-oceano-pacifico.html
2. www.politicamentecorretto.com/index.php?news=2331
3. *Panthalassa,* exhibition catalogue with critical review by Dores Sacquengna, Artlife Gallery, Arti Visive, 53rd Venice Biennale, Venice, Italy, September 2009.
4. "L'evoluzione storica della coscienza: il passaggio della Soglia"
("The Historical Evolution of Consciousness: The Passage of the Threshold"), John Peccarisi.
Milan: Il Nuovo Mondo Edizioni, 2006.
5. Vol. VI, "La terra senza il male. Jung:dall'inconscio al simbolo" ("The Land without Evil. Jung: The Unconscious to the Symbol"), U. Galimberti. Milan: Feltrinelli, 1984.
6. "Studi sull'alchimia. Il segreto del fiore d'oro e altri scritti" ("Studies on Alchemy. The Secret of the Golden Flower and Other Writings"), CG Jung. Turin: Bollati Boringhieri, 1988.
7. Vol XII "Psiche e Teche. L'uomo nell'età della tecnica" ("Psyche and Tech. The Man in the Age of Technology"), U. Galimberti, Feltrinelli,1999.
8. "Studi sull'alchimia. Il segreto del fiore d'oro e altri scritti" ("Studies on Alchemy. The Secret of the Golden Flower and Other Writings"), CG Jung. Turin: Bollati Boringhieri, 1988.

DRIFTERS

Pam Longobardi

South Point is about as far away as you can get from anything else in the United States. It stands at the mouth of the vast open vault of the Pacific Ocean. If you miss the tiny atolls of French Polynesia, that means nothing but water lies between South Point and the next solid substrate, the ice of Antarctica. South Point is the southernmost point of the United States, and it is the southernmost tip of the Big Island of Hawai'i, the primary site of my current project.

The geographic isolation and sparse population of the Big Island suggests an idyllic paradise of thriving tropical beauty. So the walloping impact of a first sighting of the vast amounts of marine debris that washes ashore here initiates a crumbling of the image of Arcadia. Marveling, as a decorator crab or a bowerbird, or a crow might, at the vast army of color, form, complexity, history, the visual impact of an initial encounter occurs in two stages. First, there is a spark of pure retinal pleasure: multitudinous bright colors and bold shapes of plastic objects, pile upon pile of tangled textural knots of driftnet, in scales that boggle the mind, from golf cart- to whale-size. A split-second later the mind processes what the eyes see and, with a sickening thud, there comes the recognition that it is our garbage, the residue of our everyday life, the quotidian castoff.

Somewhere north of the Hawai'ian Islands lies an enormous stew of ocean and plastic, described as anywhere from the "size of the state of Texas"[1] to "the size of the continent of Africa."[2] Even though the sheer enormity of this "Eastern Garbage Patch"[3] would suggest shocking aerial photographs and LANDSAT views, none seems to exist. The Patch is as elusive as it is vast, probably due to the low density of particulate matter at this scale of ocean surface. However, its sinister nature becomes amplified by this lack of visual representation; envisioning this foul broth is left to the devices of our imagination.

The Garbage Patch exists because of the efficiency of a particular current called the North Pacific Subtropical Gyre. The Gyre sweeps, in clockwise motion, south down the coast of the Americas, east across the upper Arctic frontier, north along the coast of the Asian continent, and back westward towards the Hawai'ian Islands. Its rushing force collects and carries the vast amount of floating marine debris, the majority (up to 80%) of which originates on land.[4] Flushed in from landfills, city streets, and thoughtless dumping, through vast storm sewer networks, moving with the managed flow of rainwater, our trash ultimately enters the ocean. Whatever floats, moves, so the debris that makes its way to the Gyre is predominantly plastic, in all its multitude of forms, a mixed bag of contemporary human detritus. The floating debris can take approximately six years to ride the currents from the eastern or western continental coasts before arriving in the gyre.[5] Once in the gyre, forced into higher and higher concentration as the flotilla continuously arrives, now estimated, in some portions of the gyre, at six times the biomass of living plankton there,[6] an object rarely leaves. That is, it never leaves unless it is ingested by a salp or a jellyfish, one of the army of filter feeders that are the base of the oceanic food chain. Here, plastic enters living bodies, and is handed off in each act of carnivorous ingestion, climbing up the food chain into larger predators, including man.[7]

The Gyre is a physical place but due to its lack of cohesion and representation, it becomes a location of the mind. The gyre exists on two levels—the real and the imaginary—a

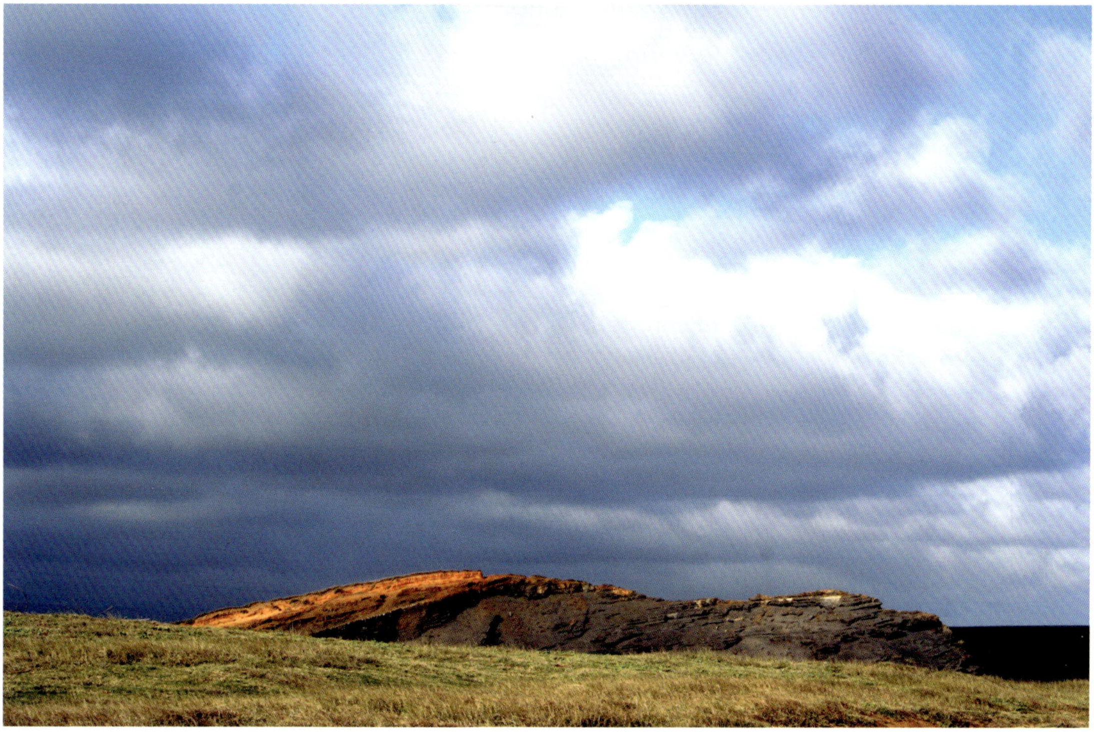

Greensand Bluff, 2006, Fuji crystal archive digital print on plexiglass, 33 x 50 in.

metaphoric swirling miasma of consumer mixture—the ultimate globality. As Robert Smithson might describe it, the Gyre functions as a non-site:

> Between the *actual site and . . . The Non-Site* itself exists a space of metaphoric significance. It could be that 'travel' in this space is a vast metaphor. Everything between the two sites could become physical metaphorical material devoid of natural meanings and realistic assumptions.[8]

The Gyre is very far from anything and difficult to get to. It is difficult also to arrive at a mental understanding of what it means. The Gyre is a very real thing that seems impossible to imagine, a non-site. The actual site we inhabit, to extend Smithson's analogy, is our everyday life. We live on land. We live in an era where industrial advancement and global consumption have made all aspects of the quotidian a matter of convenience. Convenience is marked by both materiality and impermanence. And the convenience material of choice is plastic. Quotidian objects in the world begin their journey in a state of recognition and functionality, but function and usage are stripped away through the physical and cognitive processes of time-and distance-travel as useful objects become trash. A randomly sorted collection of marine debris has its origins in functional objecthood in the same way that objective abstraction has its origins in visual culture. There can be both mental and physical processes of abstraction. Both objects and images drift between identities as the mind attempts to track their origin. The deformation processes of wind, wave, salt, and solar radiation perform a mutative abstraction to the object that functions both to remove origin and to recreate it through multiple possibilities of interpretation. Consumer products become a terrible beauty as they are transformed into marine debris. A plastic bottle becomes a toothy fossil jaw. A crate fragment becomes a Christian cross, or a Star of David.

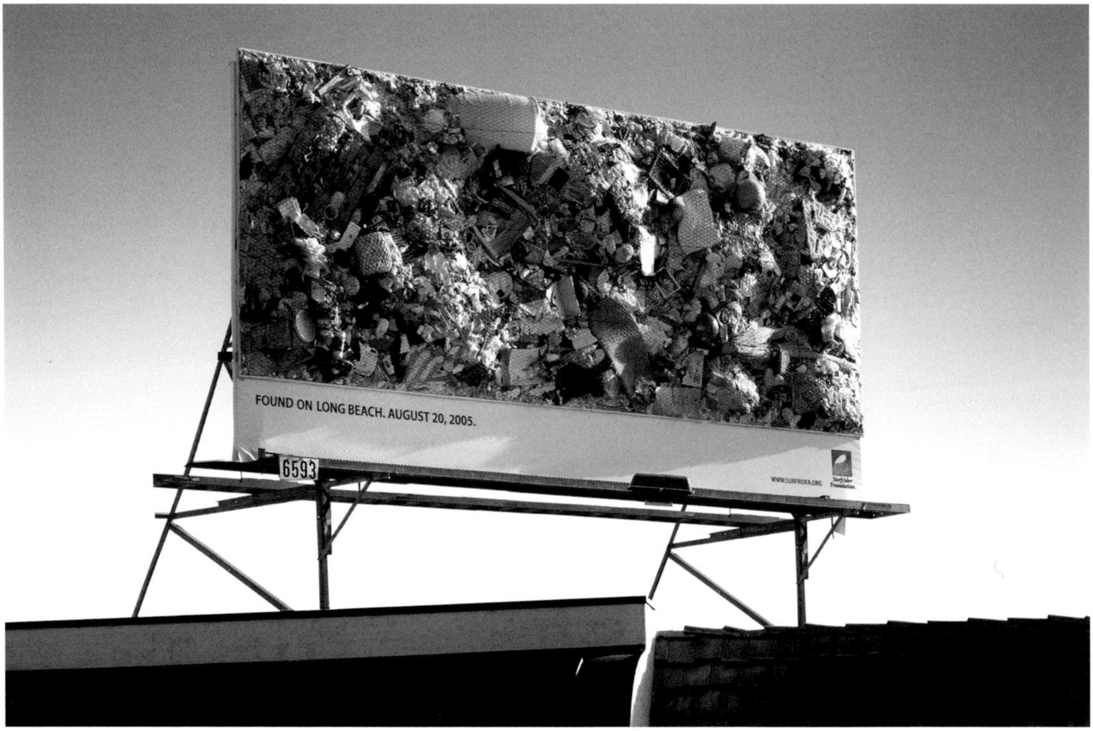

Surfrider Trash Billboard, 2005, by Saatchi & Saatchi, Los Angeles. Long Beach, California.

A container chip becomes a winking smiling face. A toy soldier and camel become limbless amputees, symbols of a protracted senseless war.
The objects themselves are castaways. At first imbued with use value, at their useful life's conclusion they are cast off and circle the globe as drifting nomads. They begin their journey at the breakfast table, in the mouth or hair, in the working hand or baby's clenched fist, the global consumer's familiar and recognizable utilitarian objects. It is at their point of transformation, into the travel-worn other, that they enter my project as *drifters.*
Drifters is the title of my ongoing project of photography, installation, and public art involving marine debris encountered at South Point, Hawai'i, and other beaches around the world. To begin, I photographically document the site as I encounter it, seeing an aesthetic of prepared installation in the deeply random course of events that leads to the deposition of the debris. The photographs of the sites on Hawai'i, in their found and untouched states, also record the poignancy of this problem, as our most pristine places on earth carry the heavy mark of human presence on the planet. I then collect and remove as much material as I can physically carry on my back, pausing neither to sort nor to classify.
My collection and presentation of these objects is a form of intervention. The intervention takes two trajectories. One is an environmental intervention that physically removes the debris material from the natural environment and resituates the objects within the cultural realm, their point of origin. The second form of intervention is a kind of freezing of the object's evolution/decay: they become freeze-framed in different states of objecthood, from recognizable to wholly mutated. I place these objects in meticulous arrangements on wall and floor and create stark photographic portraits of individual objects. These works pose a mirror in front of the viewer in that one can recognize the self and one's own participation in the creation of this materiality. Highly personal objects of hygiene and body association, such as toothbrushes and combs, are recurrent.

I also make sculptures from abandoned driftnets. Driftnets are massive vertical floating traps for fish, up to50 miles (2–90 kms)[9] long, walls of death to the unfortunate swimmers encountering them. When the nets become tangled, they are often cut loose and abandoned to drift as "ghost nets," continuing to hunt as predators. The driftnet sculptures based on web forms are called "Driftwebs." A web is also a predatory tool. The image functions metaphorically as a connection between the land and the sea to convert the discarded nets into a "trap" for plastic. It is ironic that the discarded fishing nets are now caught themselves, resituated temporarily in a different context, but never ultimately prey facing its own demise. These web-like forms suggest the interconnectedness of the web of life and our place in it.

The Great Formless

The ocean functions symbolically as the unconscious of the world, regurgitating all manner of human existence. The North Pacific Gyre acts as the eye of the ocean to record the human imprint as it gathers drifting debris in an area larger than Texas. Georges Bataille's four operations of the formless, as described by Yve-Alain Bois and Rosalind Kraus in *Formless: A User's Guide*, allows an ample platform on which to examine the conception of the *ocean as formless*, providing a further understanding of the origin of our quotidian materiality. The four operations are: 1) horizontality, 2) base materialism, 3) pulse, and 4) entropy.

Horizontality

Horizontality is a rotation implied by lowering the proud "erectness" of man, walking upright, in opposition of animal and the verticality of the animal body. The visible equals the vertical, whereas the carnal equals the horizontal.[10] The ocean is carnal; it contains the essence of the animal "other," the invisible. The vast emptiness implied by its liquid surface is the opposite of the visible or intellectual conscious. In fact, the very word that might describe the present state of awareness of the importance of the ocean is *subliminal.* Sub (below) liminal (a sensory threshold, barely perceptible,[11] below which something cannot be experienced or felt),[12] has its linguistic ties in the watery; liminal suggests the boundaries between worlds, as in a lake, above and below water. The perpetual horizontality of the ocean keeps its secrets hidden from vision; until in an act of bulimia, the ocean regurgitates the plastic it has been force-fed.

To extend the regurgitation metaphor into the real, a particular ocean-faring bird, the Laysan albatross, plies the worlds seas on air currents in search of food. The chicks, land-bound on a single group of low-laying Northern Hawai'ian Islands, await the return of the parent for the nourishing *vomitus* that sustains them. Today, nearly half the chicks never fledge,[13] as the colored bits and scraps the parents pluck from the sea are no longer crustaceans and fish, but plastic. Once plastic has floated in the ocean long enough, it becomes coated in a living algal slime that resembles the organic exterior of the creatures this bird normally feeds upon. The plastic, now regurgitated to the hungry chick, fills its belly full of indigestible, non-fortifying matter. These chicks die of starvation with a full stomach.[14] The original use-value of a functional plastic object becomes exchanged as an imposter for food.

Base Materialism

Base materialism is Bataille's counter to the idealization of matter. According to Bataille, matter is "seductive waste, appealing to what is most infantile in us."[15] Plastic is first and foremost a self-proclaiming object. In multitudinous brightly colored variforms, the innate nature of plastic is disguised as charming eye-candy. It seems innocuous, like toys. But it is not. It is dangerous.

Plastic is a biotoxin accumulator. What that means to you and me is that it is like a hard sponge that soaks up the chemical pollutants it encounters, which can be concentrated at approximately one million times the concentration in the surrounding seawater.[16] Further, a majority of these chemicals are "endocrine disruptors" that can be released when the plastic is ingested. This has caused an increase of estrogen to be found in all levels of the food chain. In fish it causes males to become female, or to fail to produce sperm. In humans, it can cause enlarged prostates, cancers, and early puberty in girls.[17] "Many of these estrogen mimics bind to estrogen receptors (within specialized cells) with roughly the same affinity as estrogen itself, setting up the potential to wreak havoc on reproductive anatomy and physiology."[18] By strange turns, the very plastic meant to appeal to our infantile selves is contributing to an ever earlier shift from child to woman, from potent to impotent.

Pulse

"Pulse" is Bois's and Krauss's term for plugging the purely optical into the libidinal. It is visual coitus initiated with no need for an image of the body to stimulate its onset. Pulse sexualizes the gaze.[19] The ocean itself has an ongoing rhythmic pulse commanded by the moon that is hypnotic to humans. The pulse of tides helps create currents, which in turn, induce the drift of ocean travel by the plastic flotilla of human flotsam. In a perverse continuation of the change of hands of commerce, these objects circle the globe on oceanic currents, plied first by trade, then by trade winds.

Entropy

For Bataille, man's gluttonous cycle of production and consumption can be blamed on the sun. "The sun expends extravagantly, forcing us into over production and waste in order to maintain even a fragile balance" with the sun's overblown expenditure. The inevitability of waste expressed in Bataille's depiction is hauntingly foreshadowed in a 1941 publication of *Science Digest*:

> This creature of our imagination, this 'Plastic Man,' will come into a world of color and bright shining surfaces, where childish hands find nothing to break, no sharp edges or corners to cut or graze, no crevices to harbor dirt or germs, because, being a child, his parents will see to it that he is surrounded on every side by this tough, safe, clean material which human thought has created . . . when dust and smoke of war cleared, plastic would deliver us from moth and rust into a world full of color . . . a new, brighter, cleaner, more beautiful world . . . a world in which man, like a magician, makes what he wants for almost every need . . .[20]

Remaking

In the 1980s, plastic was fun, ubiquitous, and largely invisible in its overabundance to the general population. When Tony Cragg used plastic in his 1980s sculptures, it was as "low" materiality. Monochromatic and figurative, any possible association with an environmental statement was smothered under a modernist blanket of form, color, and shape. As he describes in an interview with Donald Fraser, "I think that what I was interested in at that time, and that was twenty-five years ago (I'm not an artist who specializes in detritus), was to put traditional sculptural materials and even the most banal of materials on the same level. To just break down the barrier between 'noble' and 'everyday' material . . ."[21] In contrast, Portia Munson describes the dark side of material culture: "My art installations are a contemplation of and comment on our manufactured perceptions of nature. We, as a culture, are defined by the objects we mass-produce, consume, and throw away. I collect these objects and assemble them into congested installations, in essence using as my resource the refuse of consumer culture that usually ends up in landfills and yard sales, what you might call 'the backside of the mall.'"[22]
Reishee Sowa's Spiral Island, located off Puerto Aventurus near Xel Ha, Cozumel, Mexico,

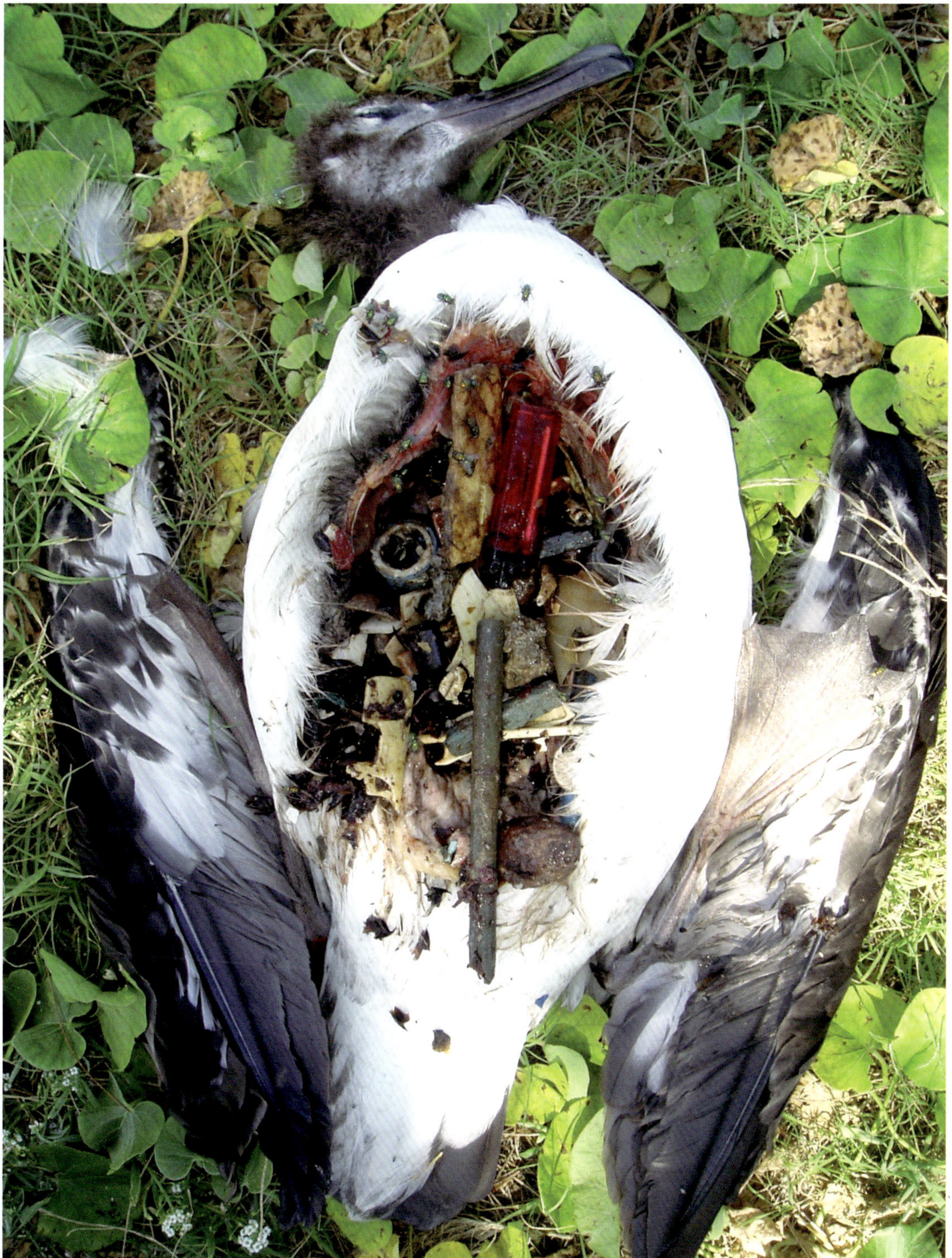

Albatross with open belly, 305 pieces of plastic found inside stomach,
photo courtesy of Claire Johnson Fackler, NOAA Office of National Marine Sanctuary.

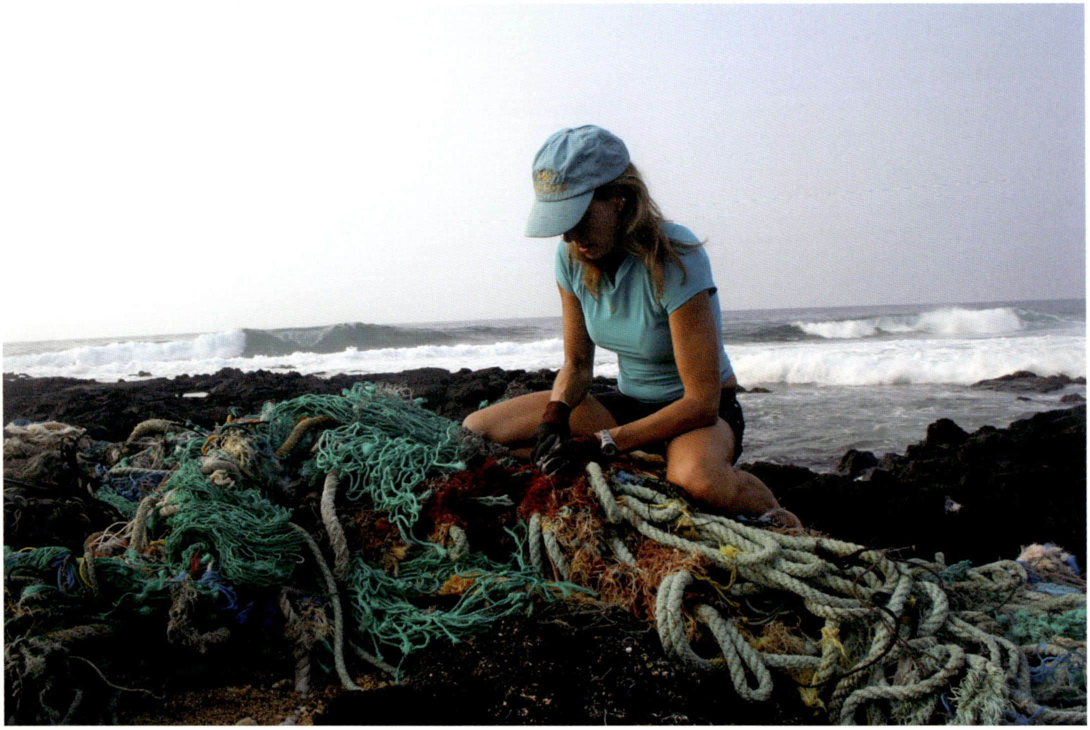

Longobardi collecting net, South Point, 2008, photo by David Rothstein.

is an ingenious construction that brings to the ubiquitous plastic bottle a final function. Begun in 1998 and taking six and a half years to build, Spiral Island "sported a two-story house, a solar oven, a self-composting toilet, and three beaches. He used some 250,000 bottles for the 66 by 54 foot structure. The mangroves were planted to help keep the island cool, and some of them rose up to 15 feet high.[23] Sowa cooked with a solar oven and even grew some of his own food. Sadly, Hurricane Emily destroyed Spiral Island in 2005, when it was thrown up on the beach, nearly intact due to the interwoven mangrove roots that grew on the island. However, Sowa has begun rebuilding Spiral Island, and as of November 2008, has 60 feet of length and a living palm tree.[24]

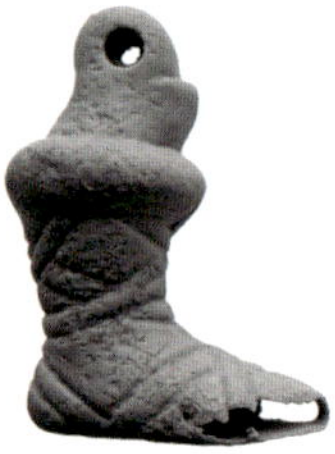

gladiatorboot, 2009,
digital photographic portrait of marine debris.

Surfrider Foundation, one of the largest environmental activist groups in the world, recently commissioned the advertising firm of Saatchi and Saatchi to create the Garbage Billboard.[25] Strung with the actual debris collected in a single day at Redondo Beach, California, this is the single best use of billboard space I've ever encountered, conflating visual pollution with actual pollution. Andrew Hughes photographs beach trash in Cornwall, United Kingdom, with an eye towards monumentalizing it, like some gigantic modern sculpture. It is, in a way. Fabiano Barretto completes the cycle by collecting and returning all plastic debris that arrives on the coasts of his native Brazil where he can determine its origin, to the parent company producer. He literally mails the errant trash back to its original owner. In my own unscientific survey, the most prevalent word I recognize, where a label can be read, is Nestlé.

The *Drifters* project continues my ongoing investigation into the psychological relationship between humans and the natural world, the physical processes of natural forces acting upon the materials I use, and a desire to create a picture of ourselves so that we may see ourselves more clearly. As a portrait of global consumer society, plastic is the hallmark of our age, the very substance of our everyday; the quotidian mainstay in endless repetition. Once valuable materials of the earth, now rare, are increasingly being replaced with plastic substitutes, which do not decay, do not biodegrade, and are becoming poison sponges in the waterways of the world. I am intending this work to be a siren call, an alarm of beautiful colors and form that tells us of its dangerous self.

Future archeologists may well know our time as the Plastocene Era.[26] Joining Plant, Animal, and Mineral, we now must acknowledge a new kingdom, a Fourth Kingdom,[27] the kingdom of Plastic, an army whose members never die or decompose, and threaten to outnumber all others.

1. Deborah Zabarenko, "Plastic Trash Vortex Menaces Pacific Sealife Study," November 5, 2006, http://today.reuters.co.uk/news/CrisesArticle.aspx?storyId=N05174536

2. Algalita Marine Research Foundation, "The Synthetic Sea," DVD, 2006 and brochure.

3. Charles Moore, "Trashed: Across the Pacific Ocean, Plastics, Plastics, Everywhere," *Natural History*, 112, 9, November 03, www.mindfully.org/Plastic/Ocean/Moore-Trashed-PacificNov03.htm

4. Algalita, "The Synthetic Sea Story," DVD, ORV Alguita/AMRF/BMP, 2006.

5. Greenpeace website, www.greenpeace.org/international/campaigns/oceans/pollution/trash-vortex#

6. Charles Moore, "A Comparison of Plastic and Plankton in the North Pacific Central Gyre," *Marine Pollution Bulletin*, 42, 12, December 1 2001, cited on www.mindfully.org/Plastic/Moore-North-Pacific-Central-Gyre.htm

7. Susan Casey, "Our Oceans Are Turning Into Plastic, Are We?" p. 4, online: www.bestlifeonline.com/cms/publish/travel-leisure/Our_oceans_are_turning_into_plastic_are_we_4.shtml

8. Robert Smithson, *Selected Writings*, "A Provisional Theory of Non-Sites," www.robertsmithson.com/essays/provisional.htm

9. Earthtrust website, "Driftnetwork Program," www.earthtrust.org/dnw.html

10. Yve-Alain Bois and Rosalind Krauss, *Formless: A User's Guide*. New York: Zone Books, 1997, pp. 13–40.

11. Miriam-Webster online dictionary.

12. Microsoft word dictionary entry.

13. Kenneth Weiss, "Plague of Plastic Chokes the Seas," *Los Angeles Times*, August 2, 2006. (Of the 500,000 albatross chicks born here each year, about 200,000 die, mostly from dehydration or starvation.)

14. Carl Safina, *Eye of the Albatross*. New York: Henry Holt and Company, 2002, p. 278.

15. Ibid., p. 31.

16. Algalita Marine Research Foundation DVD, "The Synthetic Sea Story," ORV Alguita/AMRF, 2006.

17. Algalita Marine Research Foundation brochure, "Plastics Are Forever!"

18. Trankina, Michelle, "The Hazards of Environmental Estrogens," 2001, World and I, online website, www.worldandi.com/public/2001/October/ee.html

19. Bois and Krauss, *Formless: A User's Guide, Op. cit.*, p. 31.

20. V.E. Yarsley and E.G. Couzens, "The Expanding Age of Plastics," *Science Digest*, 10, December 1941, pp. 57–59, as quoted by Donovan Hohn, "Moby Duck," *Harpers*, January 2006.

21. Interview with Donald Fraser, online www.thepander.co.nz/art/interviews/dfraser3.php

22. Portia Munson, artist statement on website www.portiamunson.com/home.html

23. www.ottawakin.ca/ckf2002/island.htm and www.playamayanews.com/article235.html, September 15, 2004.

24. www.spiralislanders.com

25. http://www.surfline.com/surfnews/article.cfm?id=1492

26. Helen Chellin, via email conversation.

27. *The Fourth Kingdom*, 1938, Bakelite Corporation promotional film, and Susan Freinkel, *The Fourth Kingdom*, title of forthcoming book, via email conversation.

THE AGENCY OF OBJECTS

Ron Broglio

It would be rather obvious to say these objects gathered by Pam Longobardi for her project *Drifters* are themselves the things set adrift. More profoundly, it is not simply them but we who are adrift in the world, and these objects remind us of our tossing about without anchor to the earth. French philosopher and cultural critic Michel Serres astutely observes, "the greatest event of the twentieth century incontestably remains the disappearance of agricultural activity at the helm of human life in general and of individual cultures. Now living only indoors . . . . the climate never influences our work anymore."[1] We are no longer anchored to the temporality of seasons nor the vagaries of the weather. We are more likely to check the weather by going online or watching television than by actually going outside, and our indoor weather is adjusted by the thermostat to seal us from nature's variability. For Serres, our fundamental crisis is that we have forgotten vulnerability in relation to nature. He suggests that we forge a natural contract with the earth in order to restore ecological order. We are in need of a way of signing such a contract and in signing toss anchor to save ourselves from this cultural drift away from the world around us. Longobardi's *Drifters* bears witness to how far we have drifted "out to sea" and provides us with material objects for thinking about a contract with nature.

By surfing along a strong Pacific Ocean current from the force of The Great Gyre, discarded everyday items make their way by the ton to the southern tip of Hawaii where they bear witness to manifold unseen and unaccounted for objects and people tossed aside in the wake of global capitalism and progress. *Drifters* strikes like the return of the repressed. All those forgotten and misshapen items come back again to tell a tale. The story they tell is of a human world of global capitalism whose economy functions by engineered obsolescence of objects and peoples. Once useful products, these drifters become castaways in a throwaway culture. Could they bear signs for a contract with nature?

If we are to sign a contract with nature, then we must do so in a language that the earth understands: "the Earth speaks to us in terms of forces, bonds, and interactions, and that's enough to make a contract."[2] The objects we toss aside are returned by ocean currents; they arrive too in the bellies of seafaring birds. Currents and corpses are a language the Earth speaks—forces, bonds, and interactions. If we read the signs of these castaway objects returned to us, we might see the contract with nature is not holding. These objects force us to rethink a more sustainable contract, one that will anchor us to the human and the natural world.

Picking among the heap of ruins that is the aborted contract with nature, Longobardi has found a number of evocative objects that reveal a failed connection with nature.[3] The palimpsest of words which read, layer upon layer, "Do Not Accept" seems like a particularly resounding refusal of nature to abide by our wish to use the seas as a dumping ground. Yet it is not simply the words which speak; it is the sheer force and mass of objects, the tons of plastic in various shapes and colors and sizes worn by the sea, which tell us something about our interaction with nature and how it has been set adrift.

Found Objects

In what is now well-rehearsed history of art, Marcel Duchamp placed on exhibition a urinal which he signed "R. Mutt 1917." He called such work "readymades" and explained

that "Whether Mr. Mutt [Duchamp] made the fountain with his own hands or not has no importance. He CHOSE it. He took an article of life, placed it so that its useful significance disappeared under the new title and point of view – created a new thought for that object."[4]
The world and its objects are redolent with meaning. To choose among them is an act of highlighting, juxtaposing, and creating. Longobardi in *Drifters* has selected a set of objects which bear witness to unseen events across stretches of ocean and over decades of time. These worn objects bear the scars and rubbings of space and time. They reveal the interaction between human culture and the relentless tides of nature. Like quasi-intelligible hieroglyphics, they speak to us of a mysterious world—of our worlds—parts of which have been repressed, forgotten, tossed aside. Longobardi's found art objects bring us to new curiosity and wonder about the seen and unseen ecology within which we abide.
Her work stands in relation to a number of artists working with the abject refuse of material culture, the garbage artists. In 1994 at the Marion Goodman Gallery, Gabriel Orozco put on display *Yogurt Caps*. James Meyers describes the artist's serendipitously found "urban detritus": "The four yogurt caps, placed at eye level on each of the gallery's walls, were ugly, ephemeral—hardly the elegant photographs and objects that one had come to expect from Orozco."[5] By selecting these clear plastic yogurt caps, Orozco makes a wry comment on the ephemeral, "plastic" contemporary culture. Unlike Orozco's commentary which maintains a distance from the object considered, Longobardi is interested in direct intervention in a space or site. One of her influences in such intervention has been the feminist eco artist Mierle Laderman Ukeles.

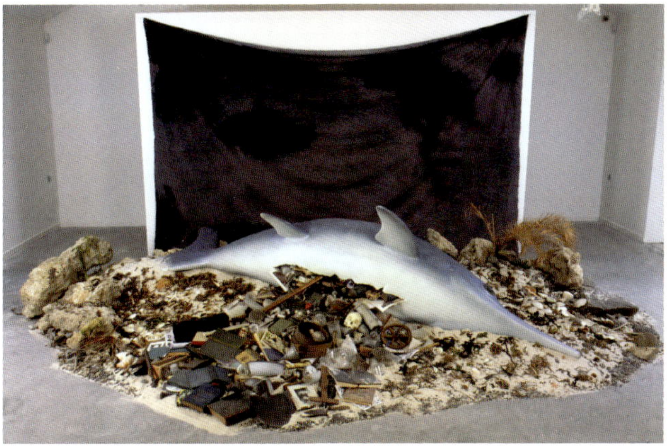

Mark Dion, Icthyosaurus, 2003.

In the early 1980s, Ukeles worked as an artist in residence with New York City Department of Sanitation. In one of her works garbage trucks are covered with mirrors which reflect back to the public its own image as seen by way of its garbage. In another work, *Touch Sanitation* (1978-1980), Ukeles shook hands with over 8,500 sanitation workers and personally thanked each of them for maintaining the city.[6] Ukeles is intimately engaged in the cradle to grave history of production of material objects and their forgotten afterlife. Longobardi's own work is a feminist and ecological intervention in recovering these repressed remains.

Hauntology

Worn by their travel, the objects appear as relics of another time, a former civilization. In fact, Pam Longobardi has brought them to the gallery as prophetic objects that are ruins of our future. Otherwise said, today's traces of petrochemical plastics afloat on overly trafficked seas tell the tale of our precarious cultural ecology and possible environmental

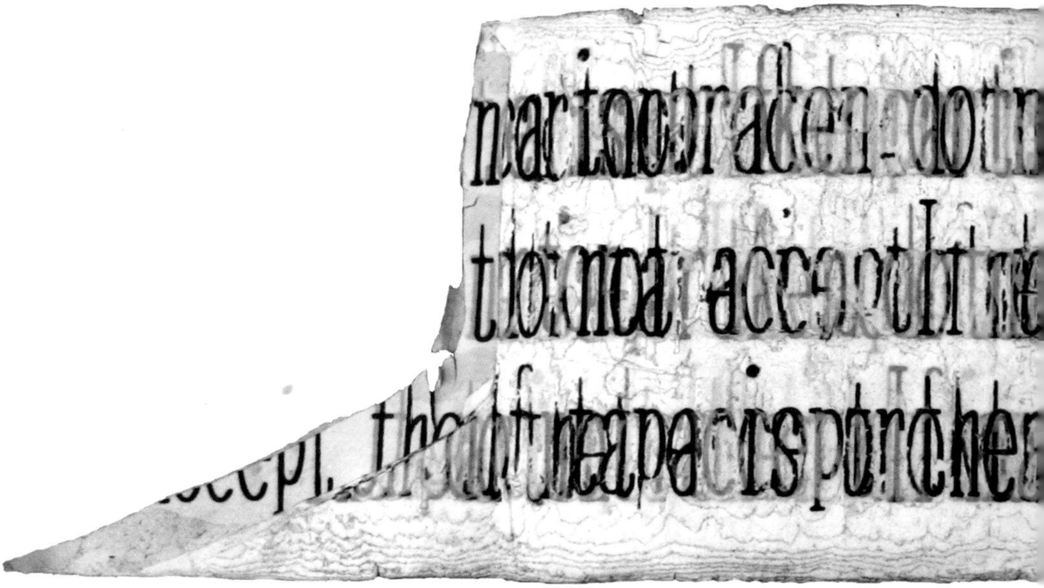

textstrip, 2008, digital photograph portrait of marine debris.

collapse. They are spectral haunting of the present from a recent past (when the object was discarded) and the unforeseeable future where threat of an eco-apocalypse sends messages to the present by way of refuse. These objects are dead and forgotten trash, but in the gallery they are brought back to life as specters. Longobardi's selection makes these talisman objects speak in hieroglyphic markings of their journey. Refuse as trash and *refuse*—do not accept—these two figures of trash and refusal haunt the shiny, modern techno-global capitalist present.

Longobardi's reconfiguration of trash relates in another way to Mark Dion's sculptures which critically evaluate techno-scientific progress and its systems of valuation. In *Icthyosaur,* Dion places a recreated version of this dinosaur on a pile of trash in a classical visual pyramid. Longobardi's *Eye Test Chart: Colorblindness (dead C red C)* uses classical round forms and the visual eye test chart to ask us to what it is that we see in these objects. Have we learned to read? Like Dion's evaluation of progress, her *Defective Flow Chart* materializes the progress of capital though detritus. Capital flow becomes the flow of sea-born refuse. Technology, science, economy and culture bear their progress by way of material objects. Longobardi manifests the material implications of conceptual work done by flow charts and the eye test charts.

The strong relationship to science (Longobardi has worked in collaboration with NOAA) and the conceptual bent in Longobardi's work places it in clear alignment with the work of Agnes Denes. Denes wrote in 1998 of breaking "through boundaries of art and deal(ing) with ecological, cultural and social issues . . . map(ping) human evolution," and creating "social structures and metaphors for our time."[7] Longobardi's interventions extract evidence for the study of ourselves and refocus the lens of a larger anthropological view of nature and culture.

Longobardi has performed her own unearthing. *Drifters* is an unearthing of our past as well

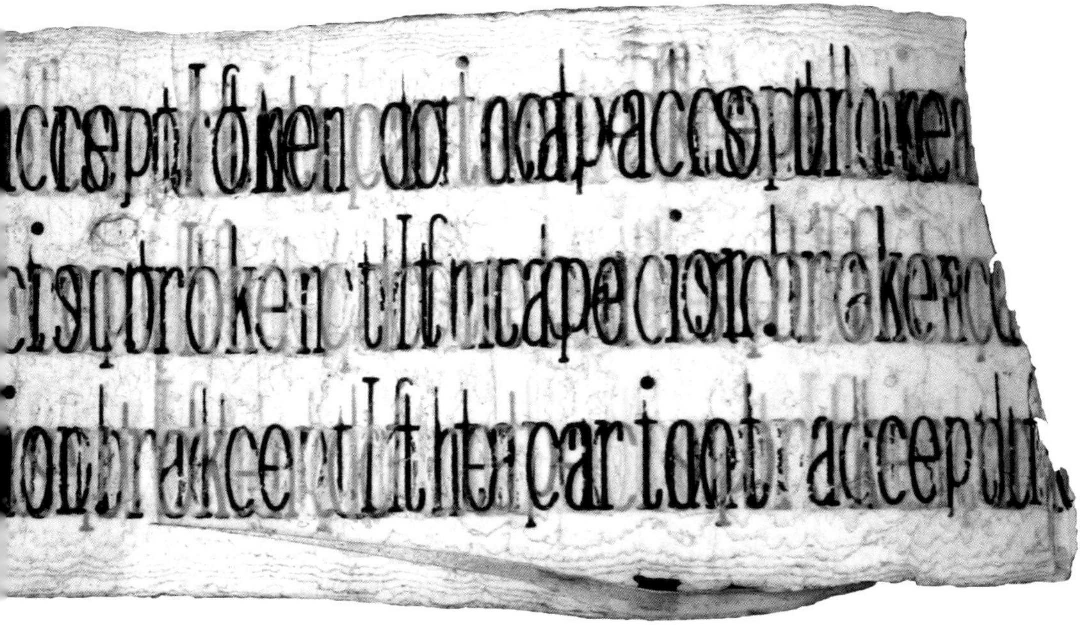

as a reflection on the state of affairs in the present. These objects are in plain sight for any who cares to visit remoter beaches of Hawaii but for most of us, they need to be unearthed—dug up and moved to visible places. In doing so, Longobardi shuttles and translates between the language of the earth—a world of forces and interactions—and the cultural language of humans. Her art moves between blunt materiality and cultural meaning. She intervenes in the landscape with the care of an eco-artist translating between worlds.

With art there is hope that we will recognize our refuse and imagine—along with the artist—a different future. By bringing global refuse transformed by the forces of nature into the gallery setting, Longobardi imbues forgotten fragments with an aura and mystery. The gallery, and now this book, provides a space of contemplation where the viewer is invited to consider ways of piecing together irreconcilable images—Hawaiian beaches, ocean waves, industrial progress and refuse.

1. Michel Serres. *The Natural Contract*. Ann Arbor: University of Michigan Press, 1995, p. 28.
2. Ibid, p. 39.
3. The term "evocative objects" here is meant to cite the collection *Evocative Objects: Things We Think With* by Sherry Turkle (Cambridge: MIT Press, 2007) and the near cousin to her work, Roland Barthes's *Mythologies* (Noonday Press, 1972).
4. *The Blind Man*, Vol. 2, 1917, p. 5.
5. James Meyer. "Nomads: Figures of Travel in Contemporary Art," *Site-Specificity: The Ethnographic Turn*. Ed. Alex Coles. London: Black Dog Publishing, 2000, pp. 10-26.
6. Holland Cotter. "That Sanitation truck Parked on the Pier? It's Part of the Show," *The New York Times*, Art Review, February 23, 2007.
7. Agnes Denes. "Sheep," *The Human Argument: The Writings of Agnes Denes*, Ed. Klaus Ottmann. New York: Spring Publications, 2008, pp. 202-204.

PACKING SLIP

1 4 9 8 7 9 7

Via

Market ID: 77075423
Order ID: 1498797
Order Date: 10/20/2026
Shipping Method:

Ship To

bris APEX DC 77075423-18
EX
AVONDALE AVE.
ANDVIEW HEIGHTS, OH 43212-3473, US

SKU	QTY	TITLE	TOTAL
SM.1DFZI	1	John T. Hill: Random Access	12.99
SM.1EWOA	1	Japanese for Busy People III: Workbook	7.05
SM.1CSQ4	1	Pam Longobardi: Drifters: Plastics, Pollution, and Personhood	15.81

Order Total: $35.85

ur order has been packaged and created with great care. Enjoy! Bay State Books

∞

sites

∞

object portraits

∞

sculptures and installations

∞

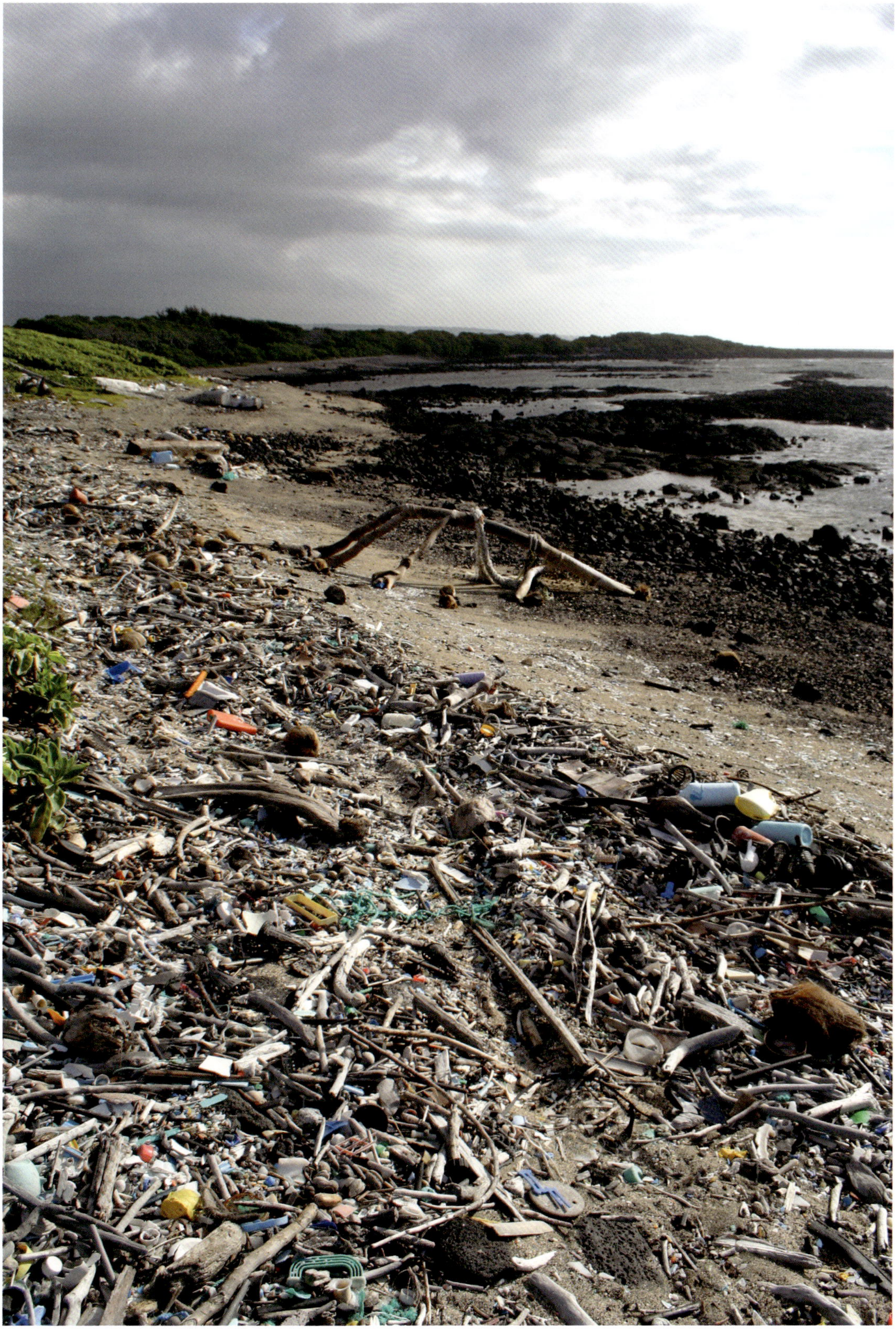

Endless Array, 2008, Fuji crystal archive digital print, 50 x 33 in.

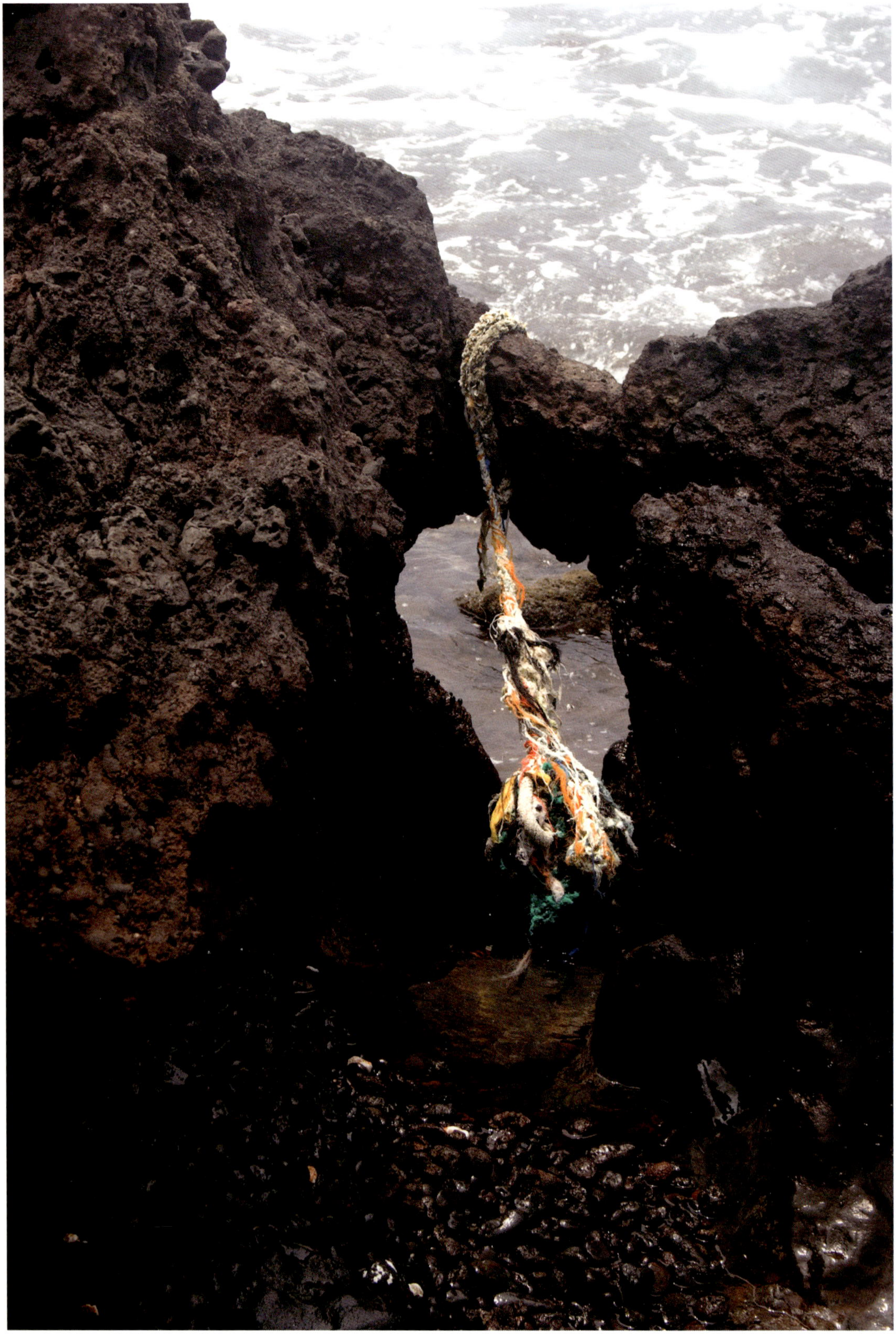

Lava Noose, 2008, Fuji crystal archive digital print, 50 x 33 in.

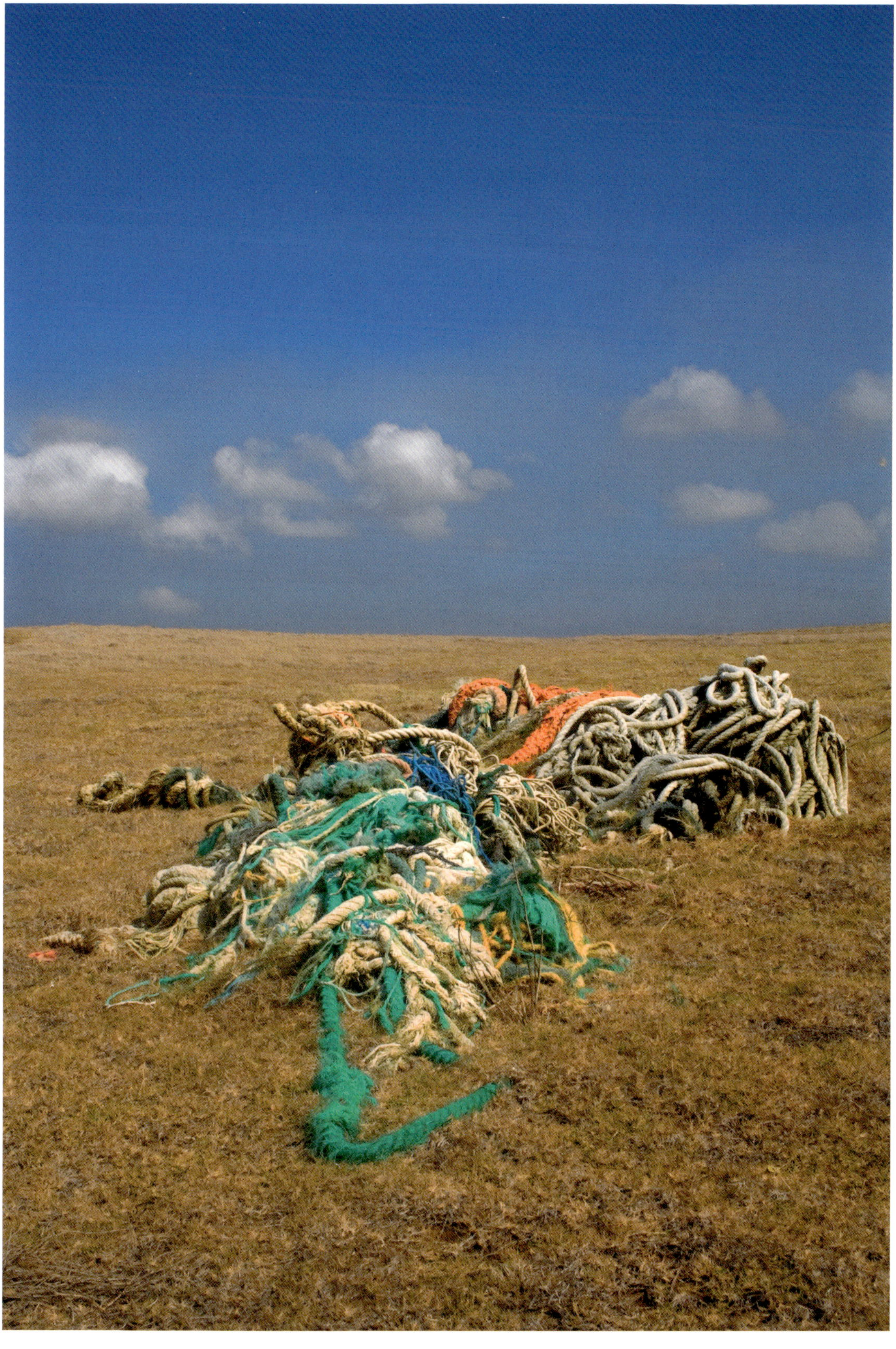

Field Net, 2008, Fuji crystal archive digital print, 50 x 33 in.

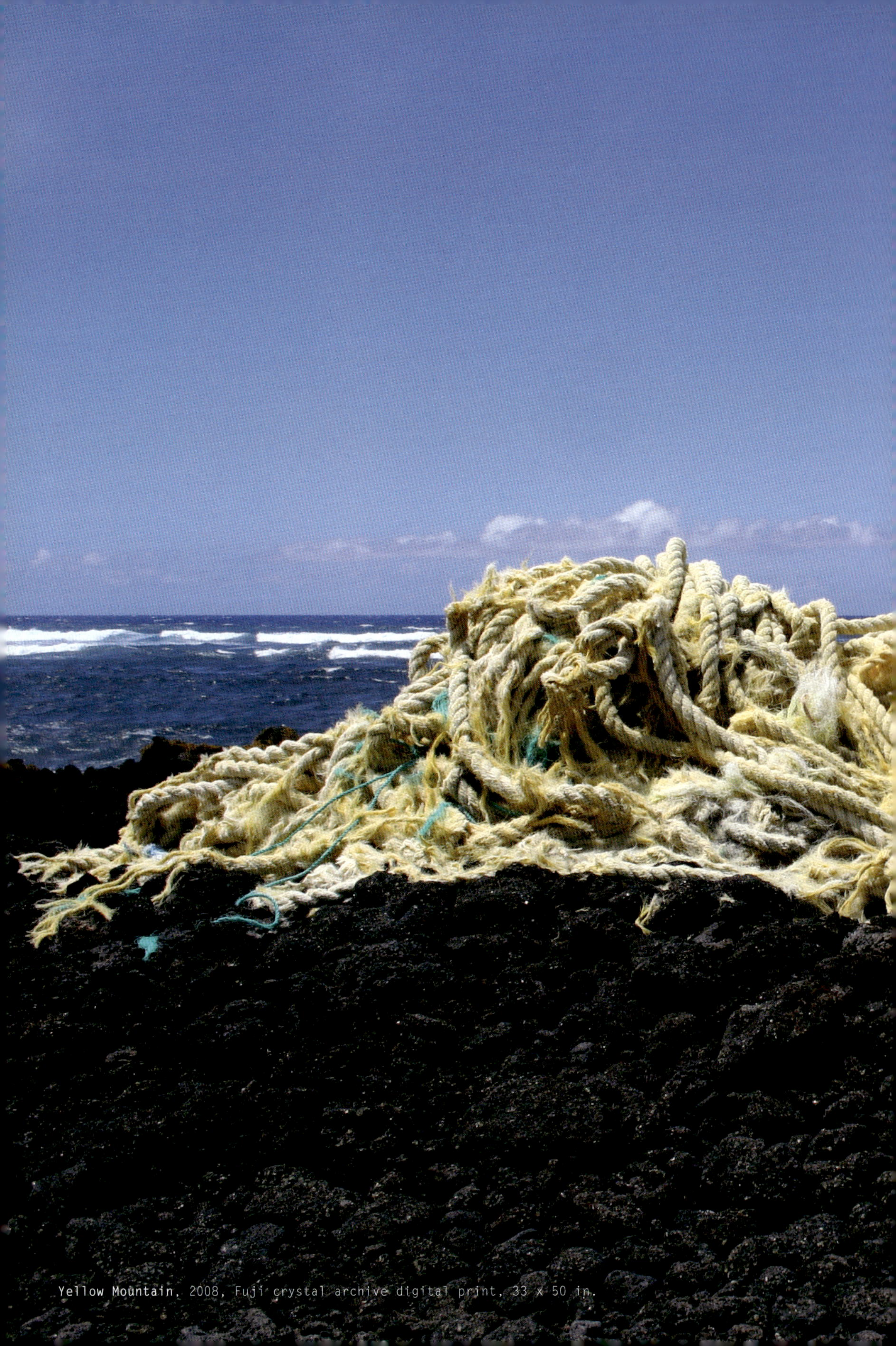

Yellow Mountain, 2008, Fuji crystal archive digital print, 33 x 50 in.

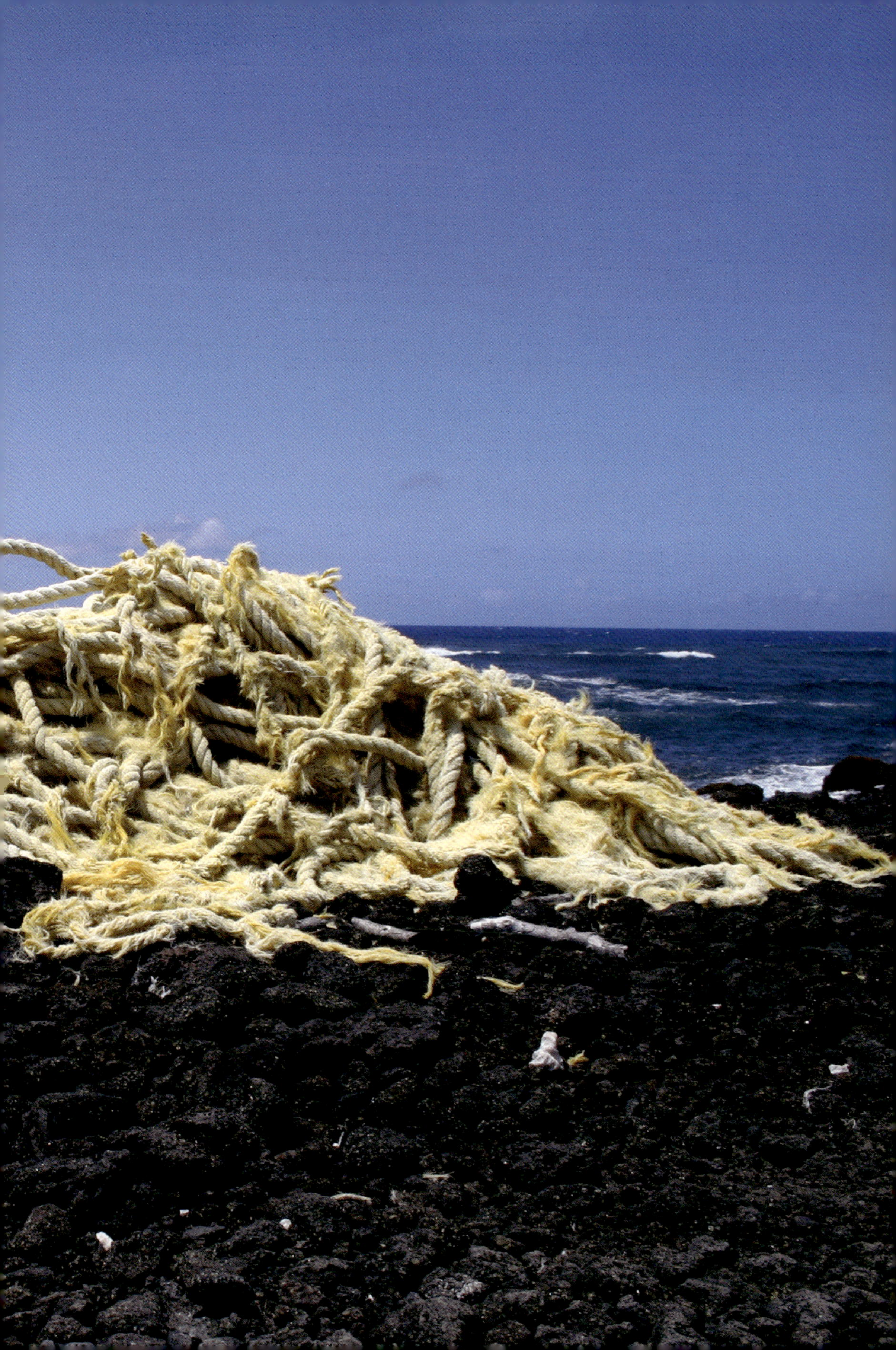

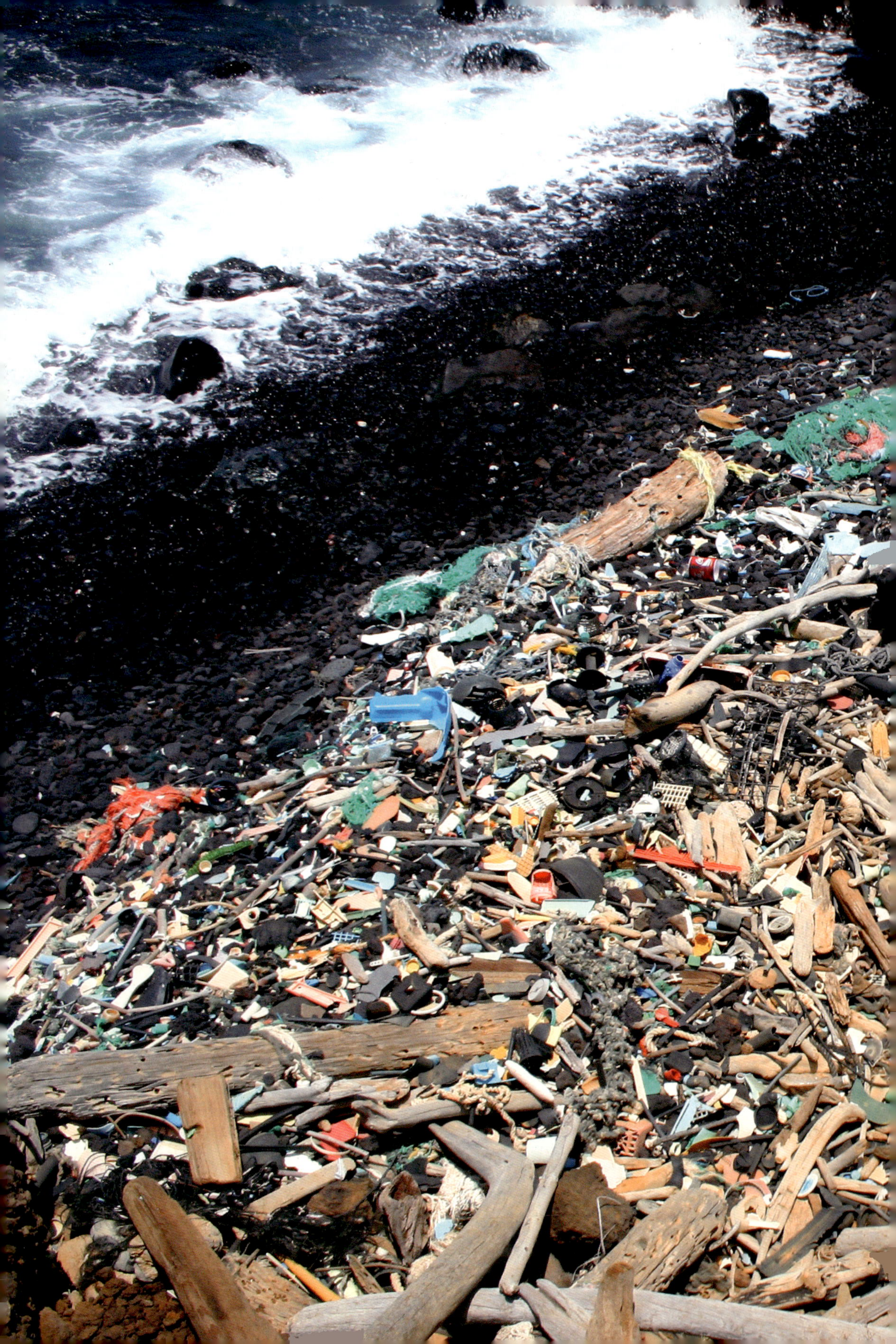

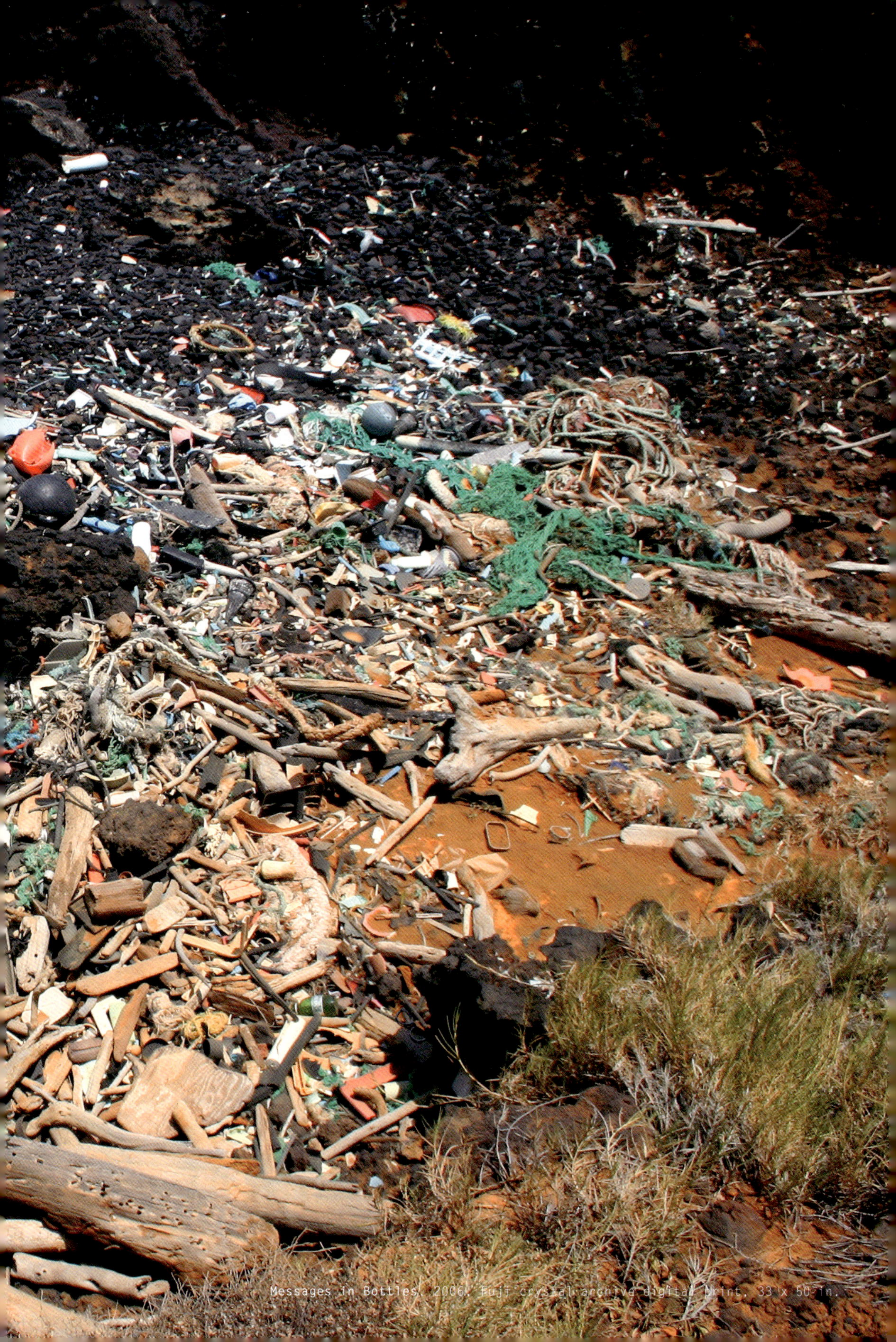

Messages in Bottles, 2006. Fuji crystal archive digital print, 33 x 50 in.

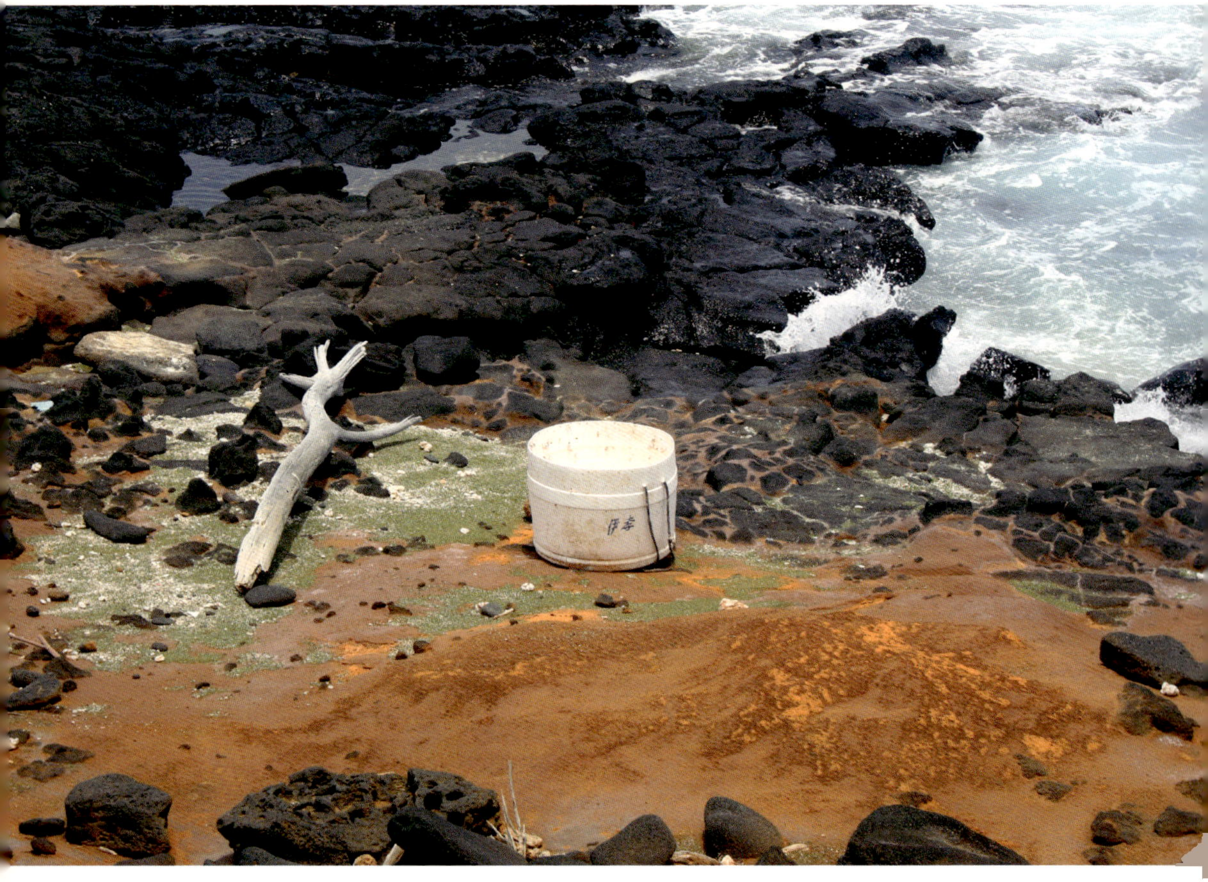

Consumption, 2006, Fuji crystal archive digital print, 33 x 50 in.

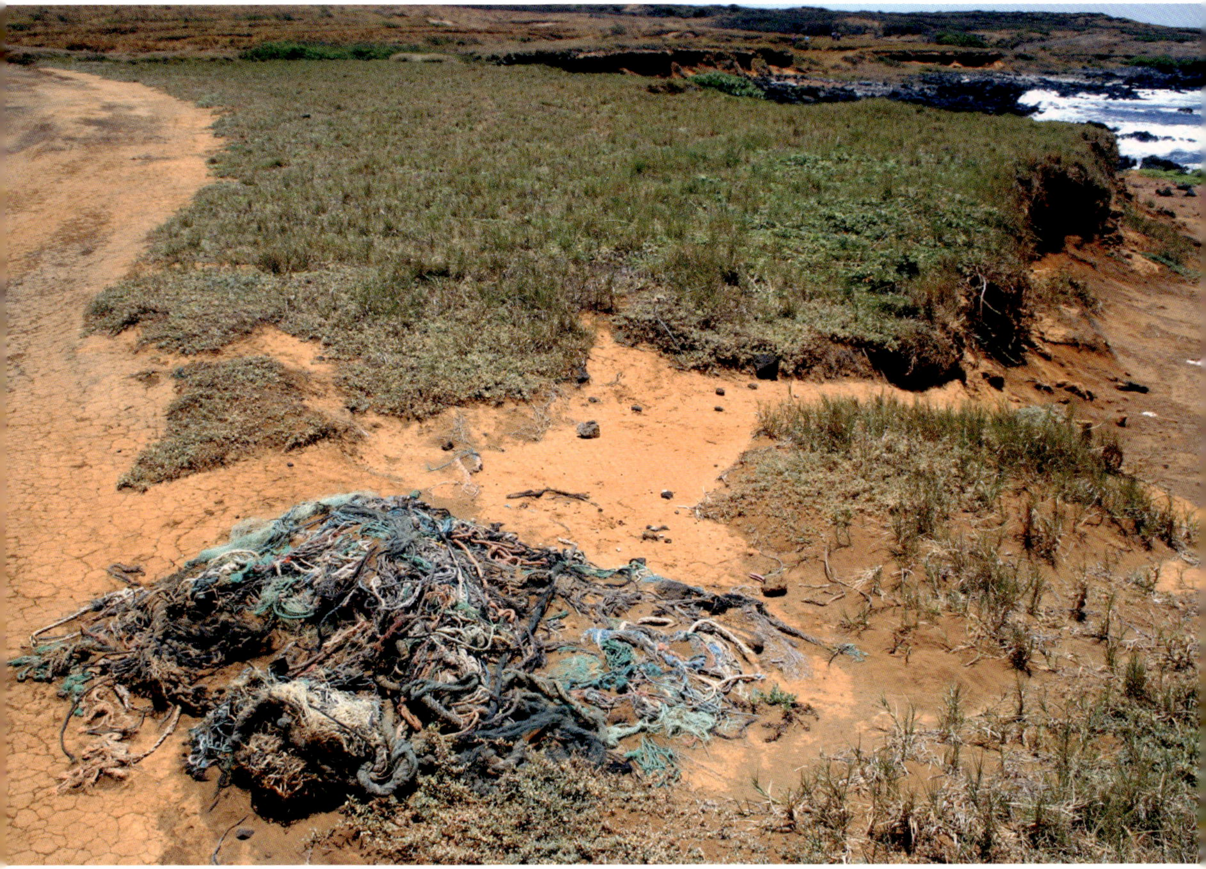

States of Matter, 2006, Fuji crystal archive digital print, 33 x 50 in.

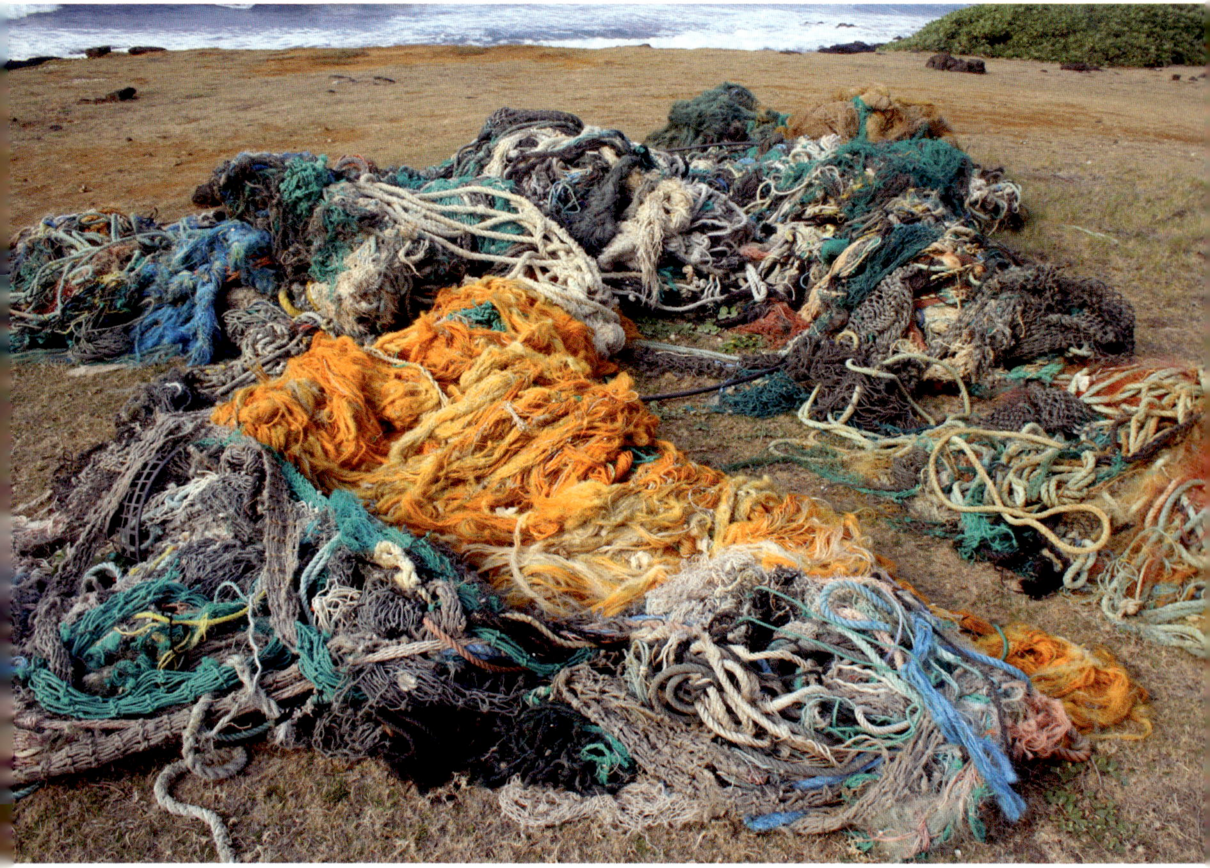

Tangled II, 2008, Fuji crystal archive digital print, 33 x 50 in.

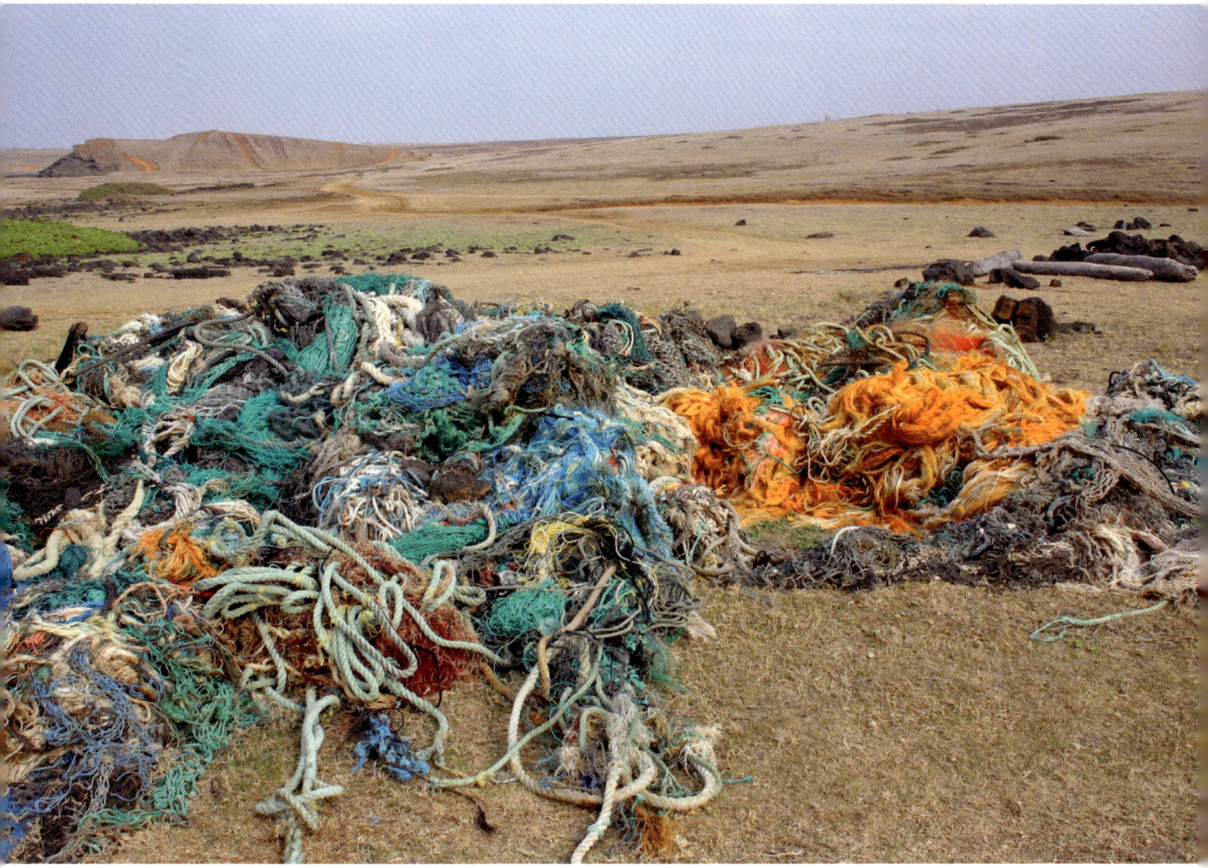

Tangled I, 2008, Fuji crystal archive digital print, 33 x 50 in.

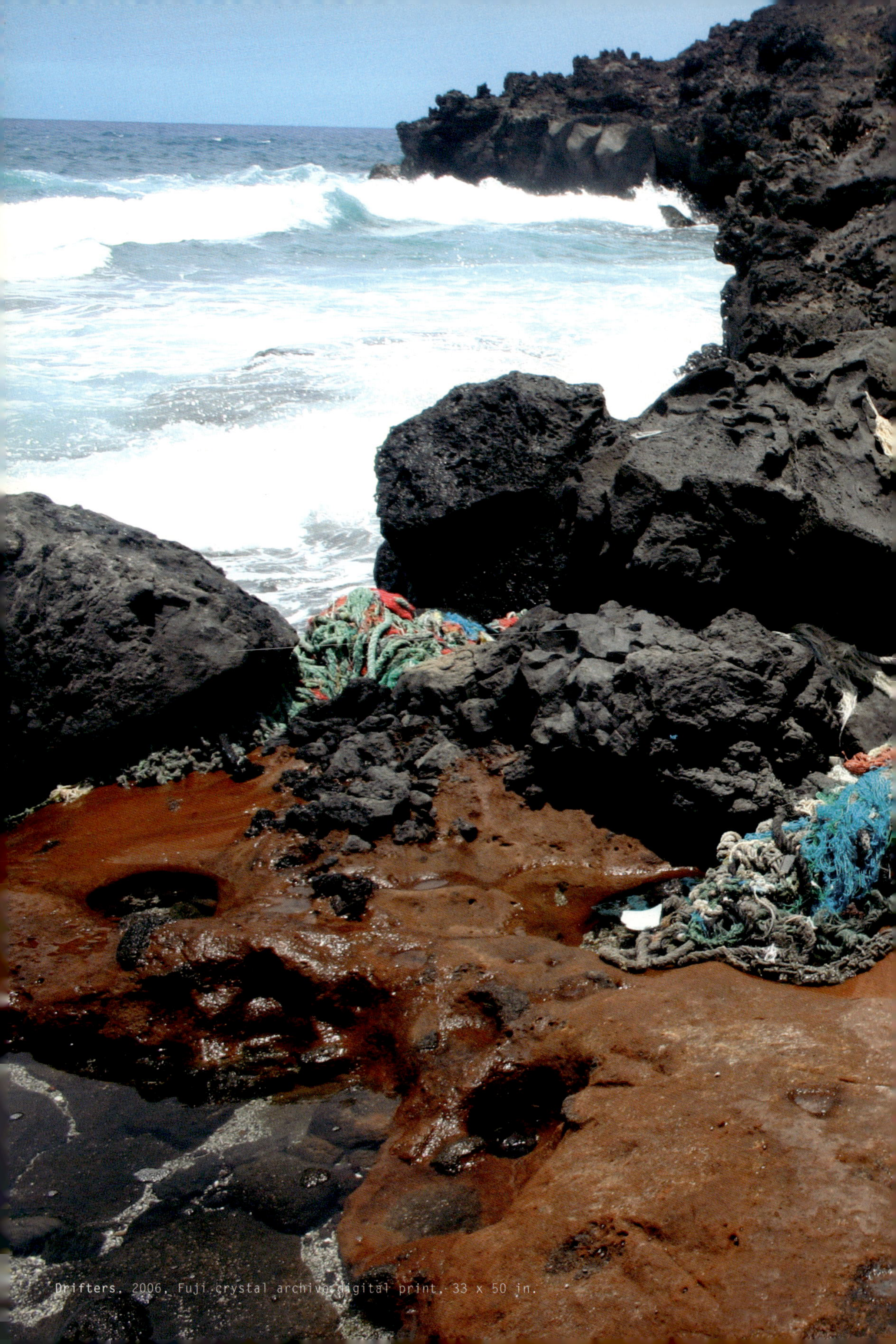

Drifters, 2006, Fuji crystal archive digital print, 33 x 50 in.

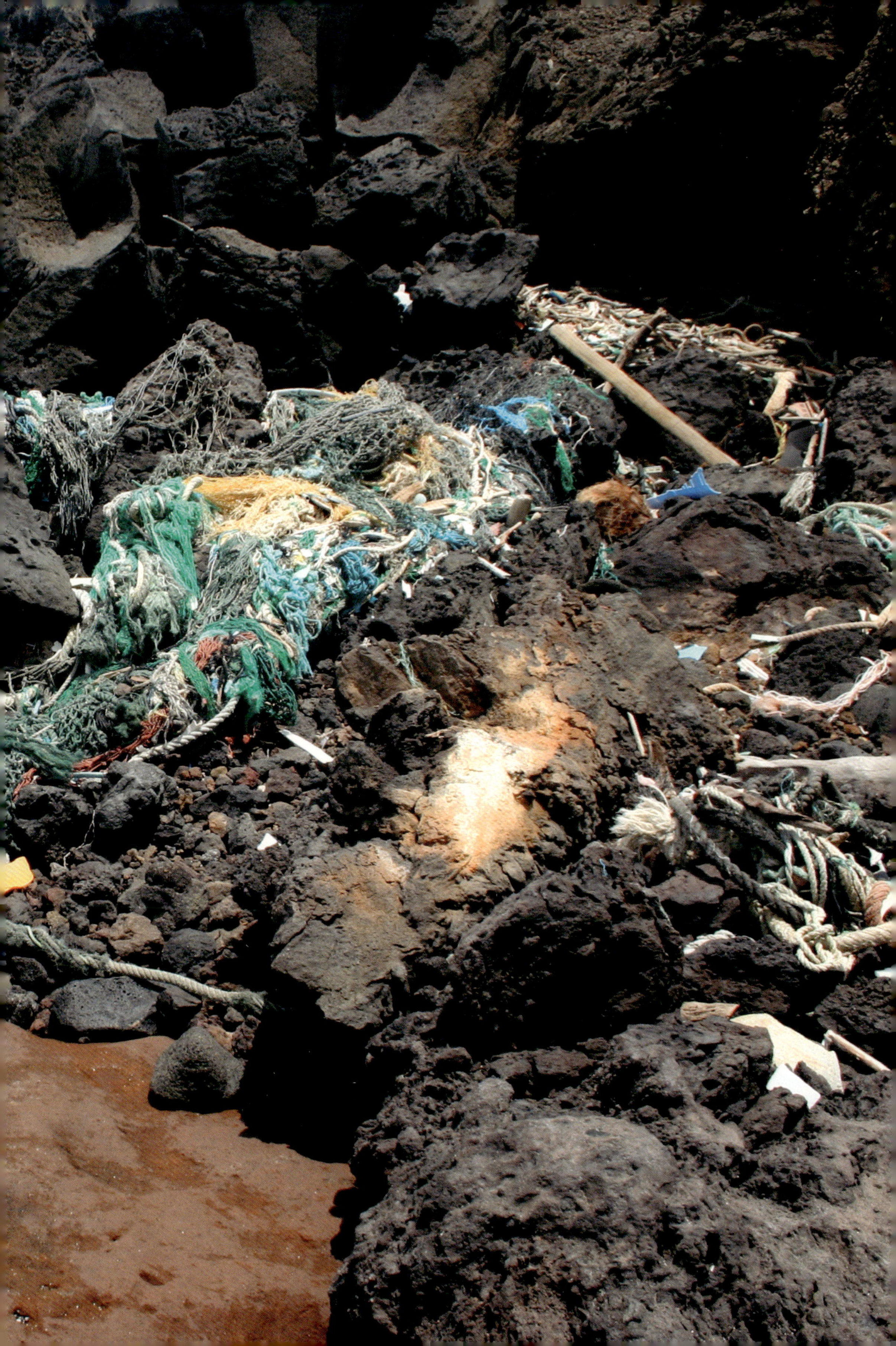

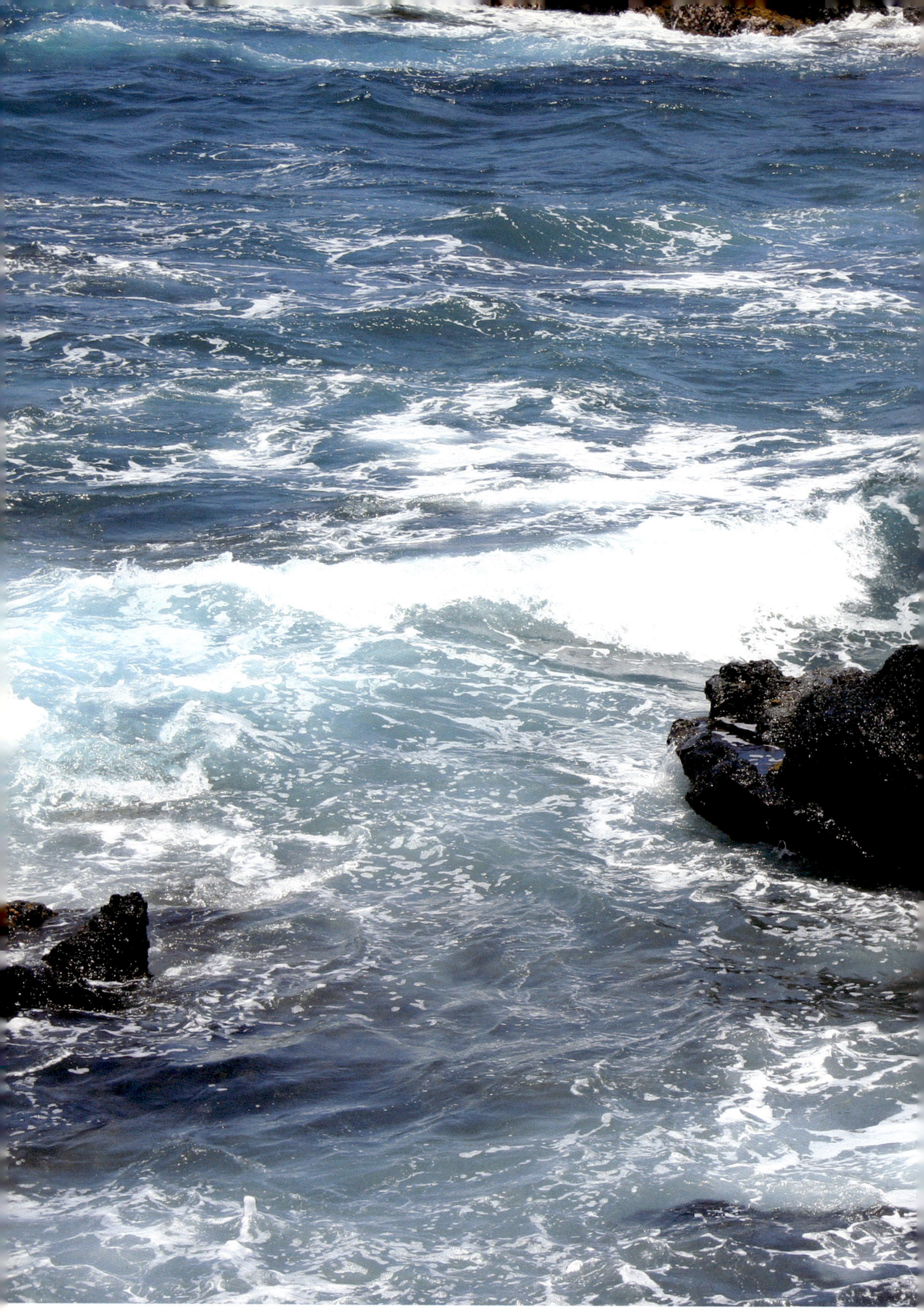

Throne, 2006, Fuji crystal archive digital print, 33 x 50 in.

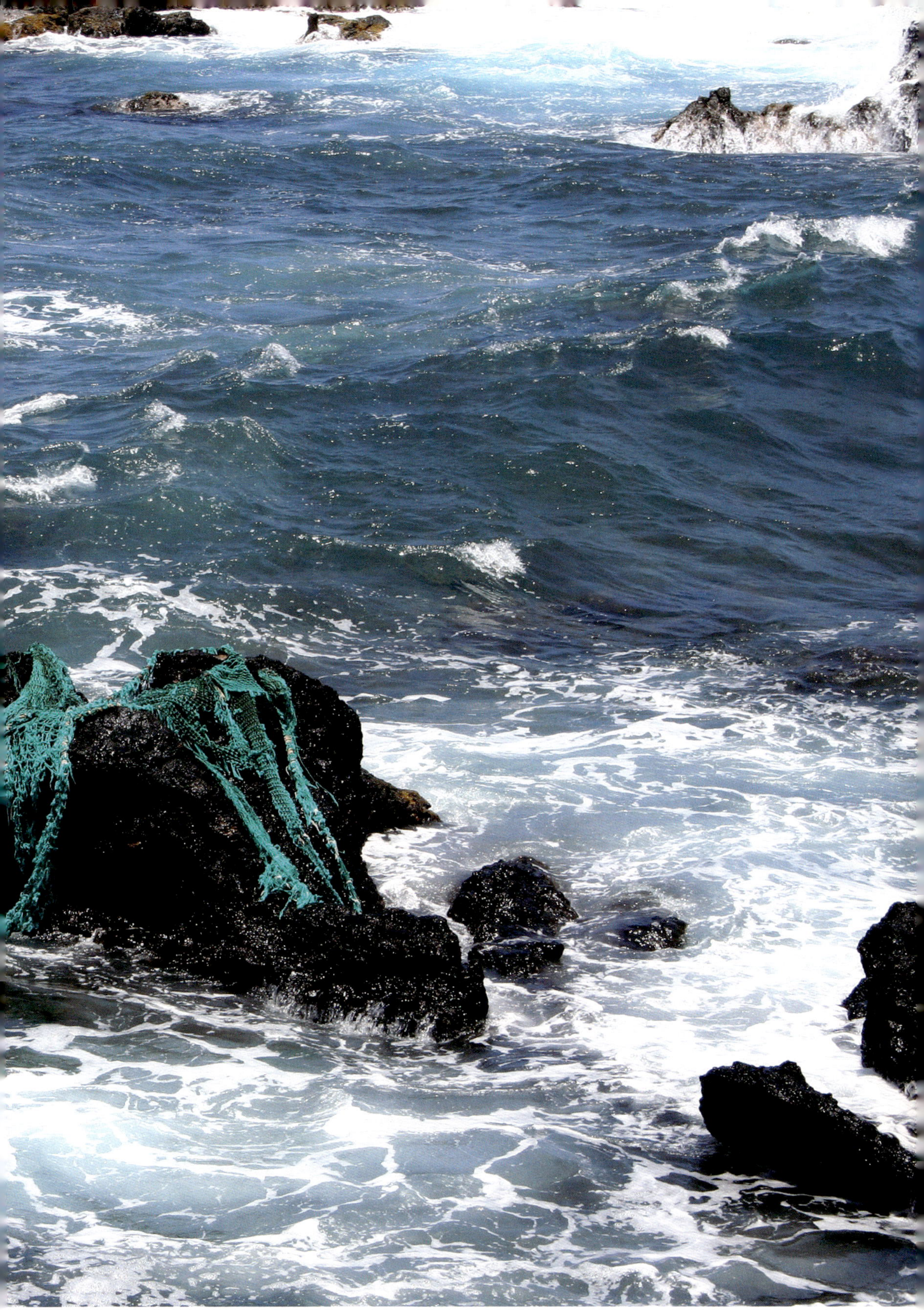

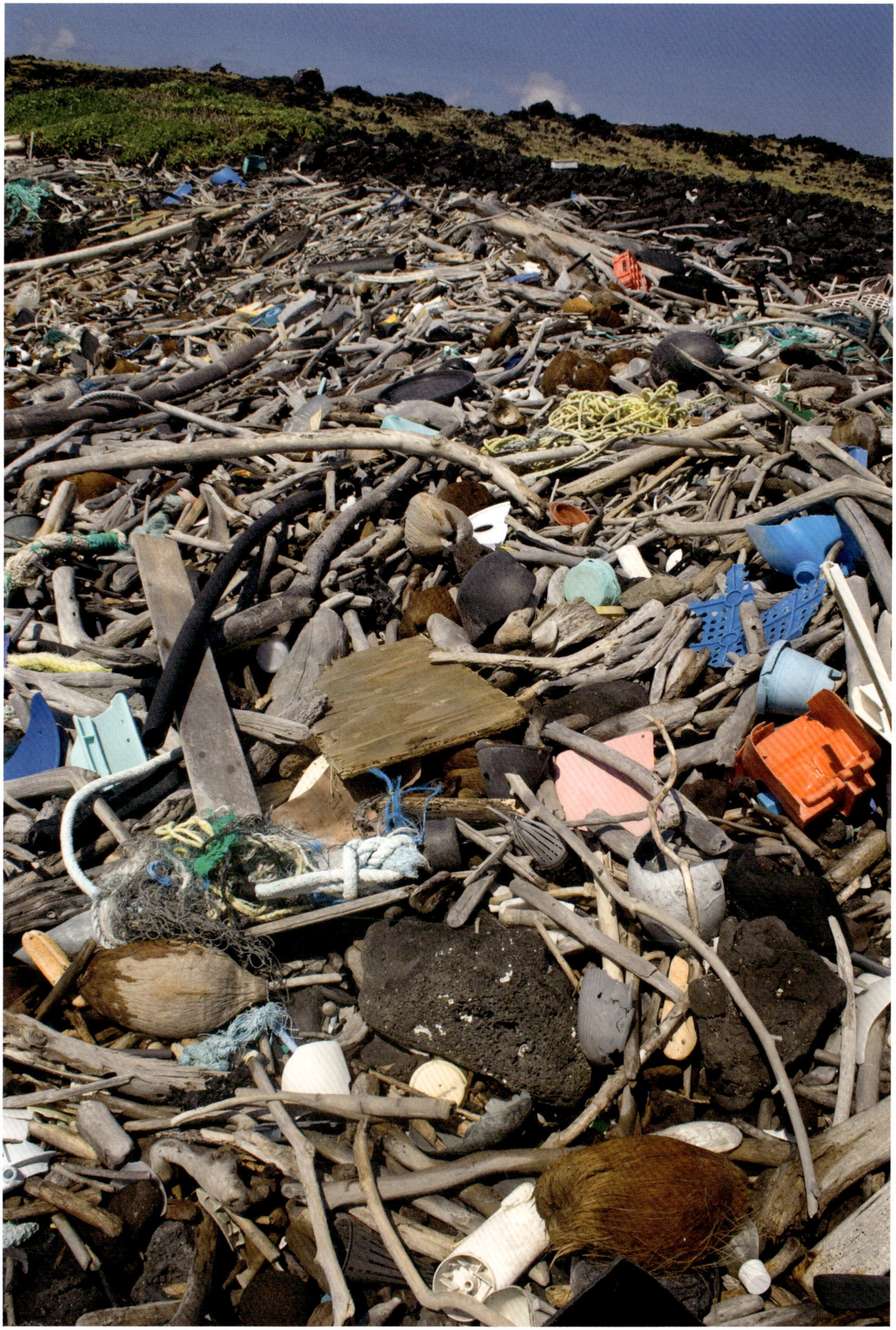

Plastic World, 2008, Fuji crystal archive digital print, 50 x 33 in.

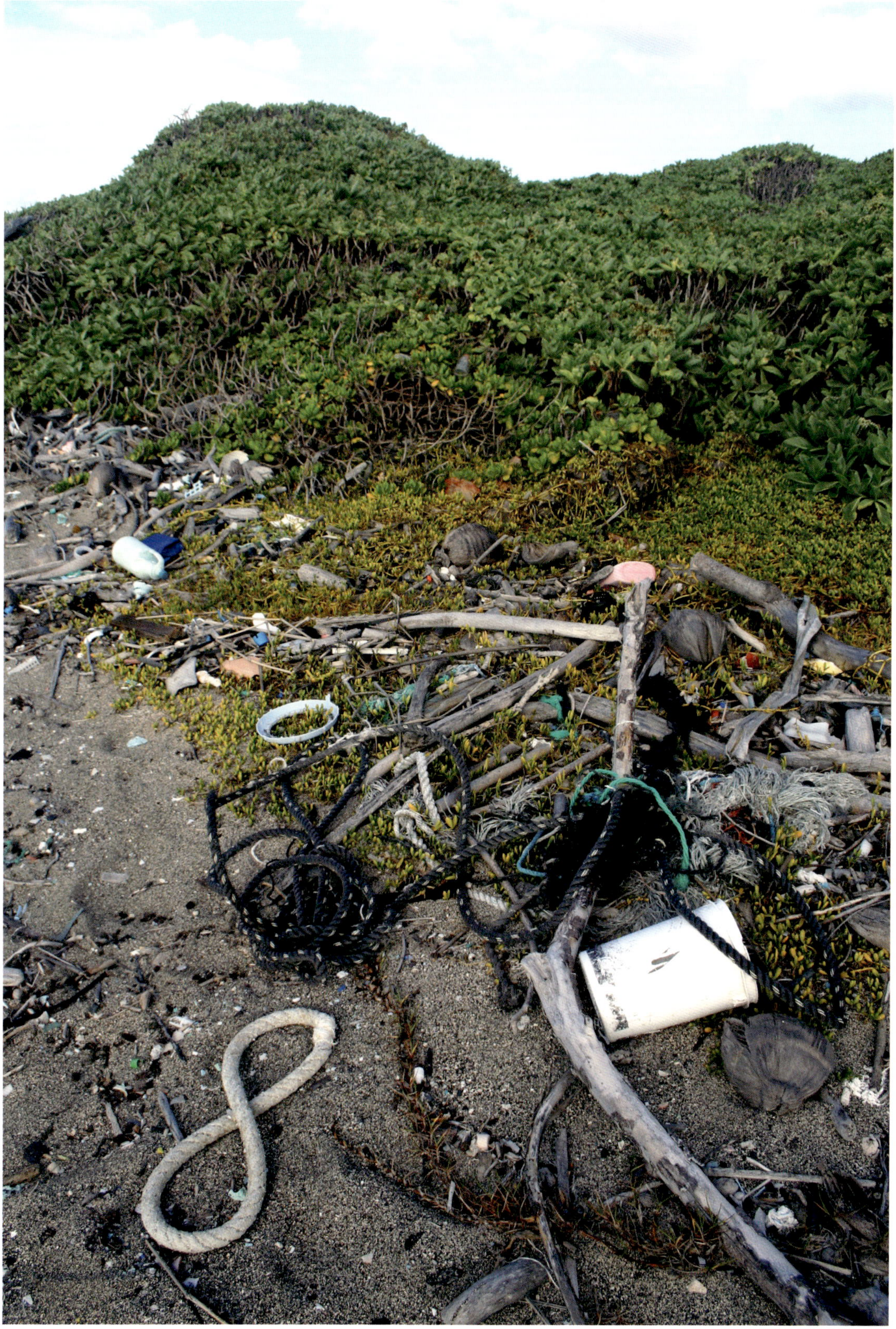

Infinity, 2008, Fuji crystal archive digital print, 50 x 33 in.

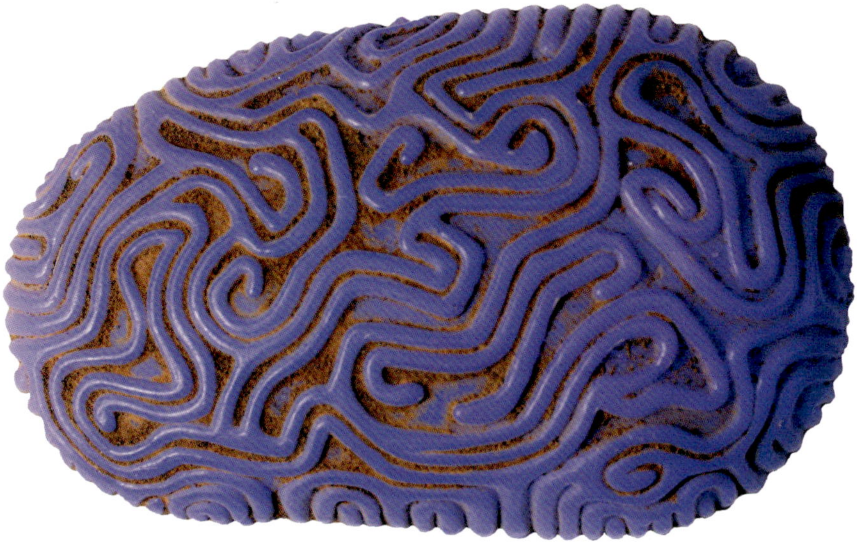

smallbrain, 2007, digital photograph portrait of marine debris.

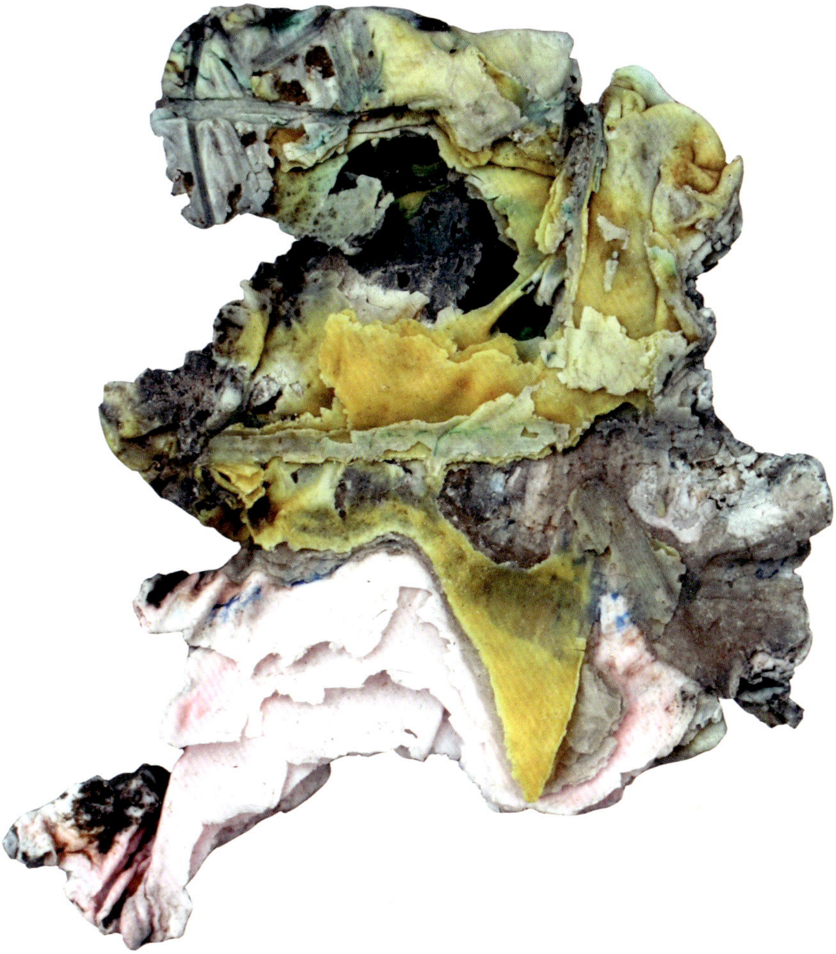

meltcolor, 2008, digital photograph portrait of marine debris.

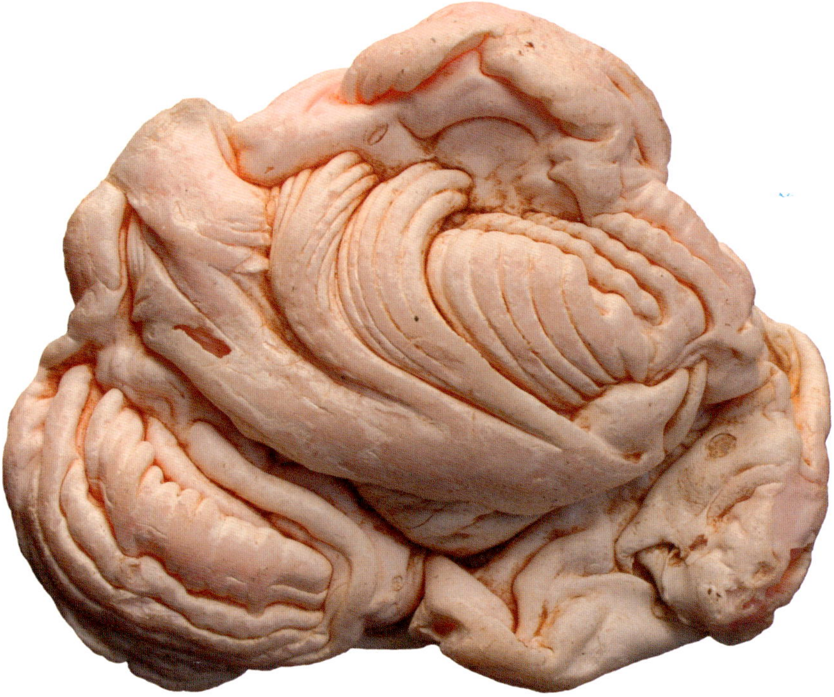

pinkblob, 2008, digital photograph portrait of marine debris.

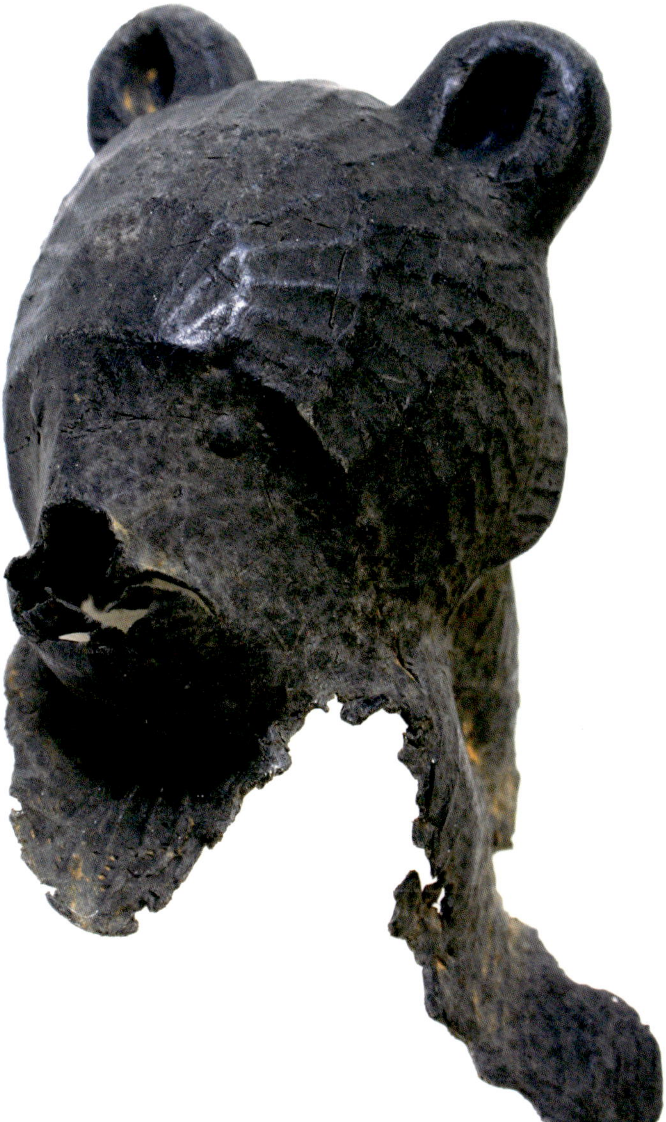

bearhead, 2008, digital photograph of marine debris.

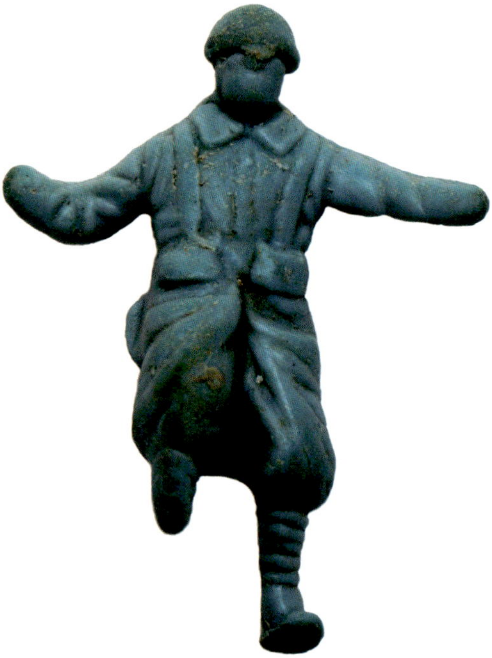

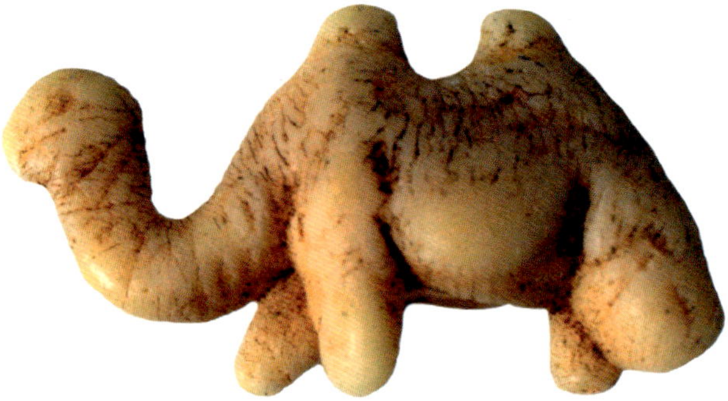

armymanblue, 2007, digital photograph portrait of marine debris.
camelnub, 2006, digital photograph portrait of marine debris.

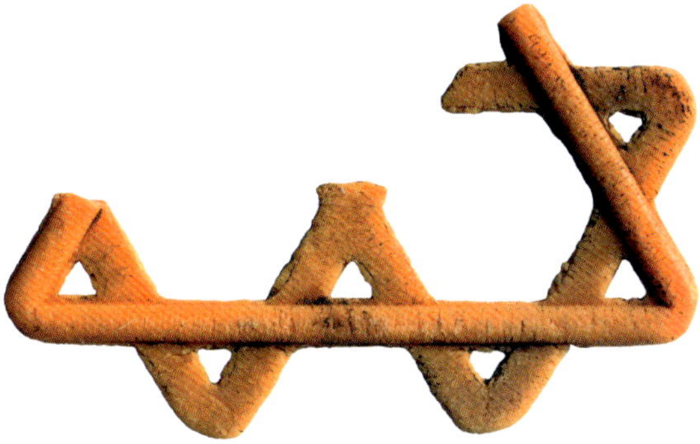

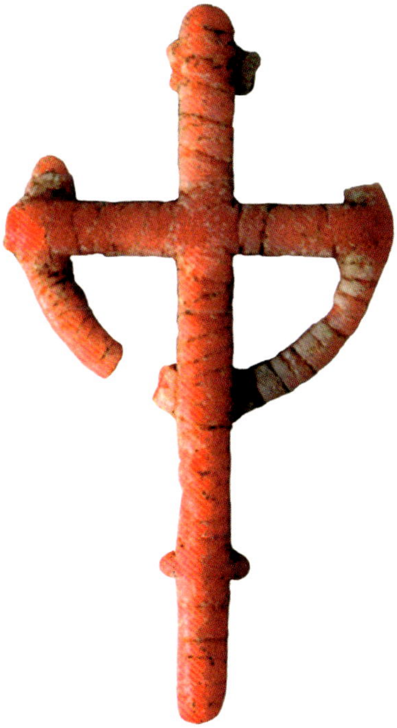

starsofdavid, 2007, digital photograph portrait of marine debris.
INRI, 2006, digital photograph portrait of marine debris.

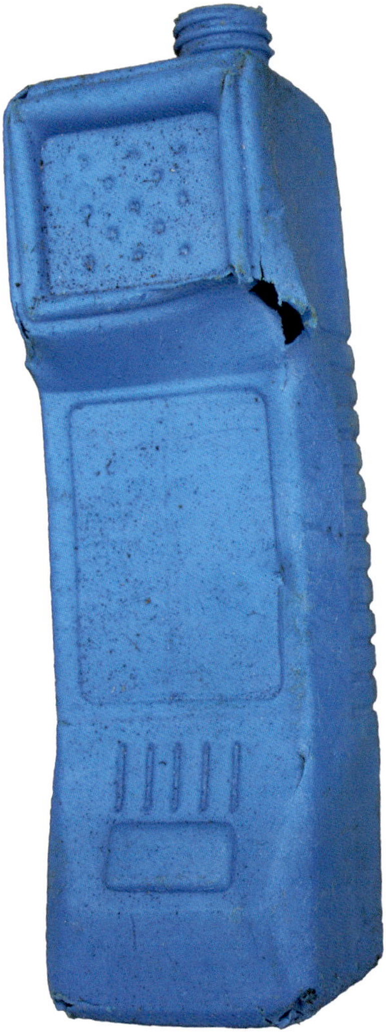

phonebottle, 2007, digital photograph portrait of marine debris.

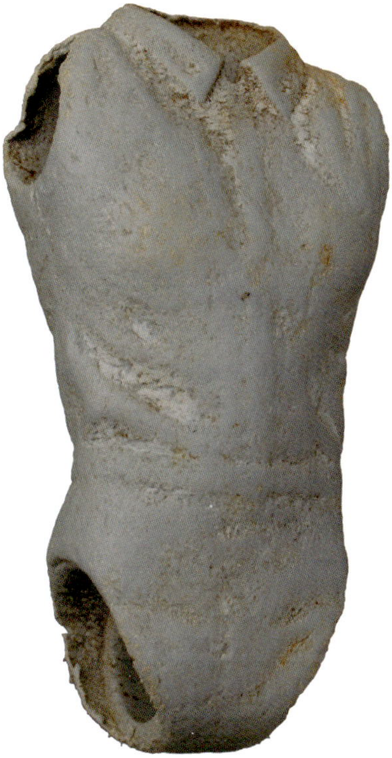

bodyguy, 2008, digital photograph portrait of marine debris.

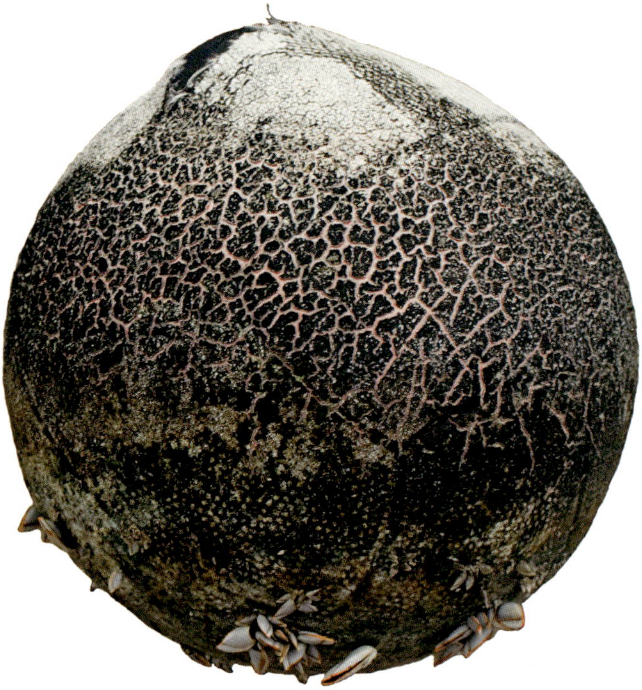

barnacleball, 2008, digital photograph portrait of marine debris.

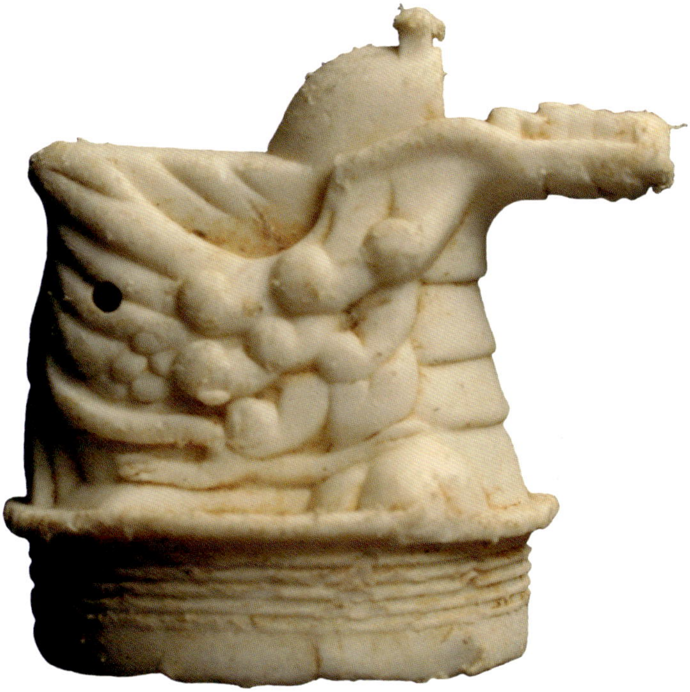

dragoncastle, 2008, digital photograph portrait of marine debris.

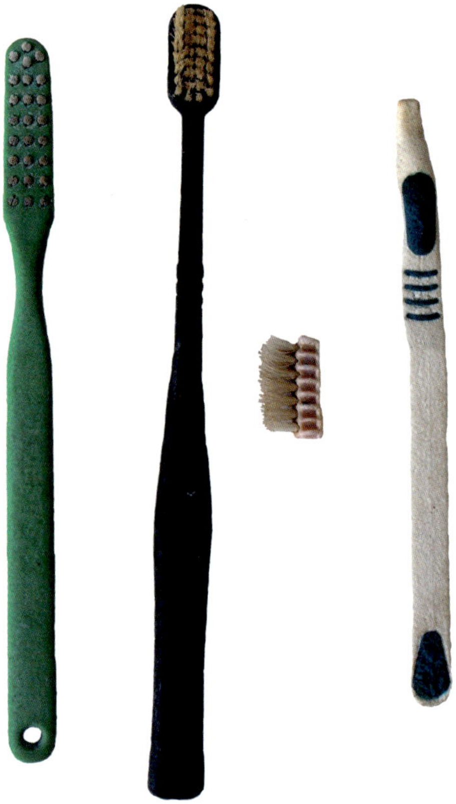

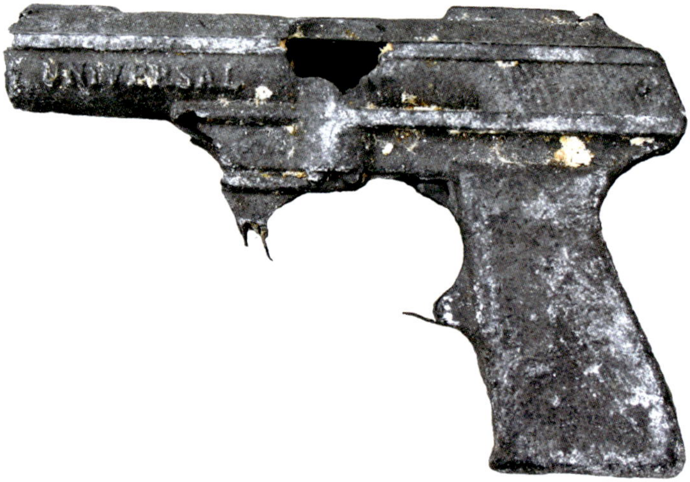

toothbrushes, 2006, digital photograph portrait of marine debris.
universalgun, 2007, digital photograph portrait of marine debris.

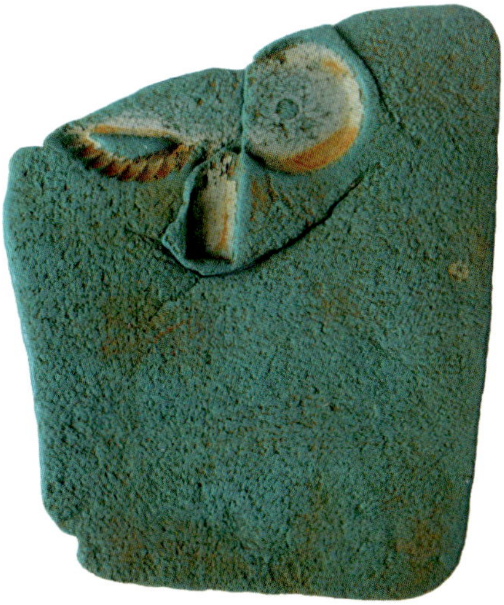

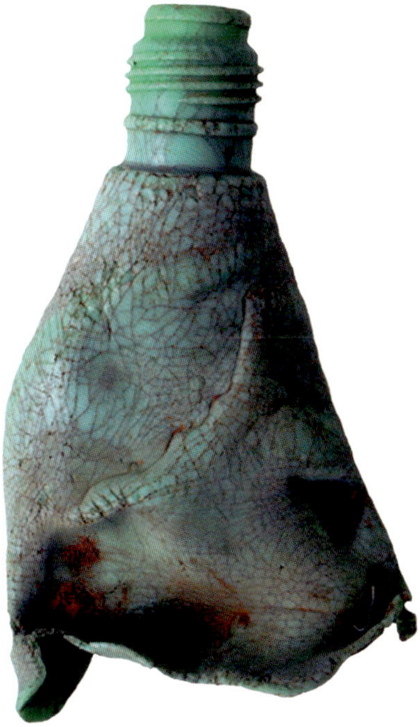

winkface, 2006, digital photograph portrait of marine debris.
crazedbottle, 2006, digital photograph portrait of marine debris.

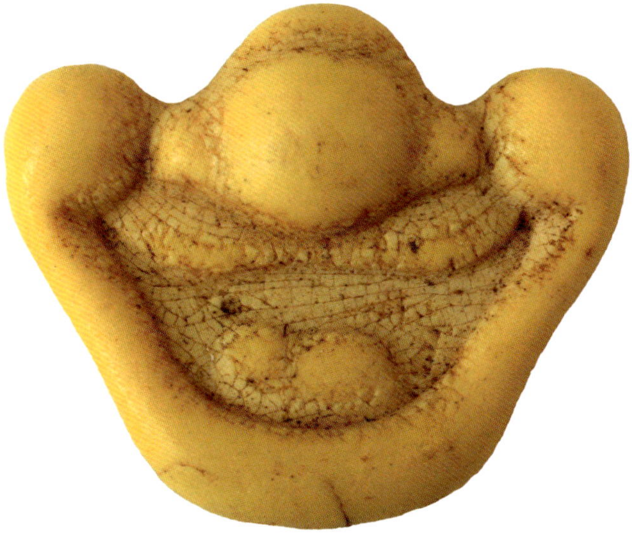

smilemouth, 2007, digital photograph portrait of marine debris.

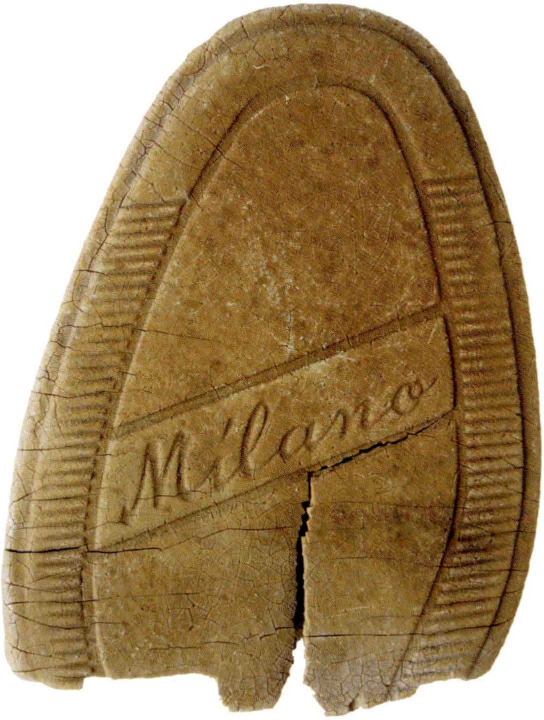

milanosole, 2006, digital photograph portrait of marine debris.

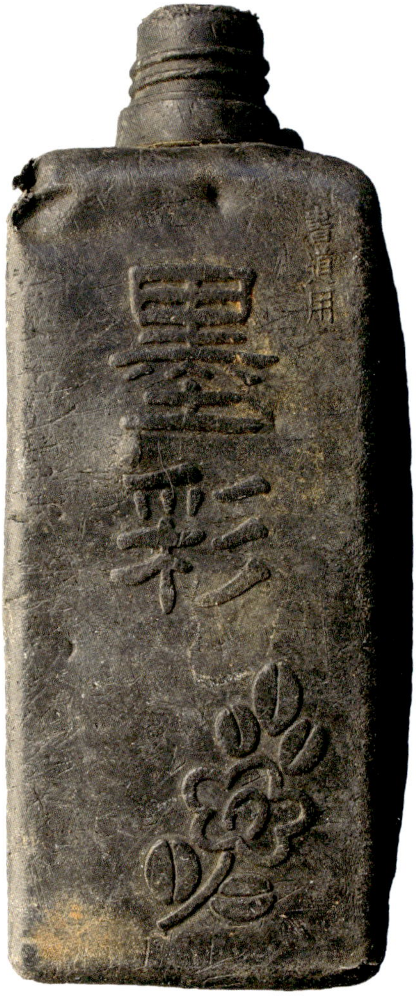

blackinkbottle, 2008, digital photograph portrait of marine debris.

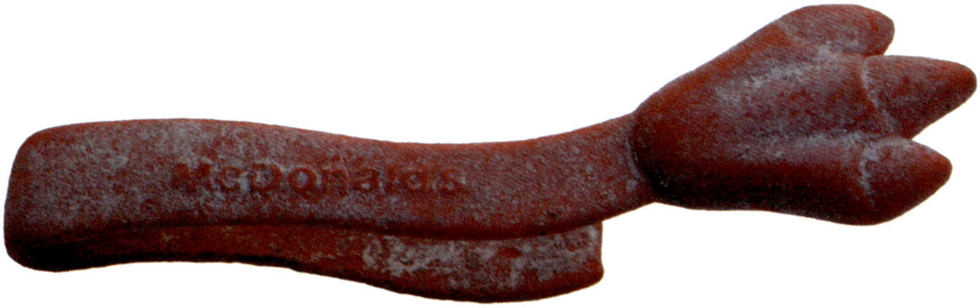

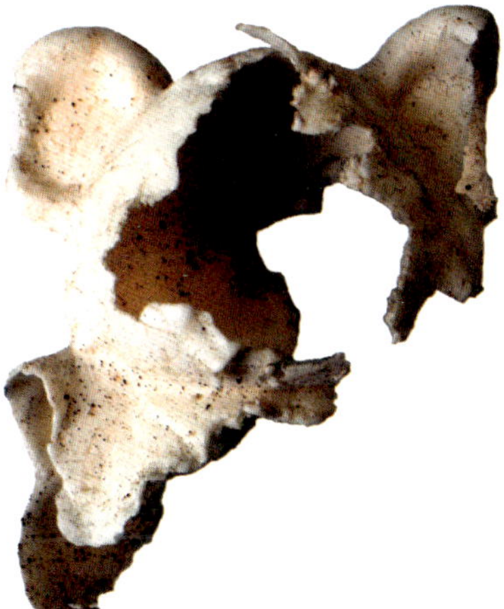

clawtongs, 2008, digital photograph portrait of marine debris.
pighead, 2008, digital photograph portrait of marine debris.

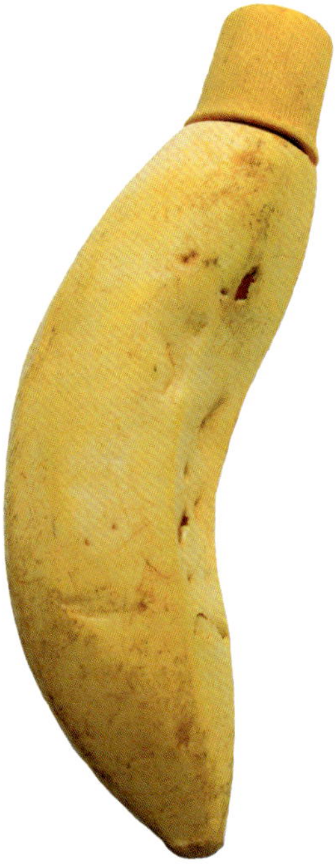

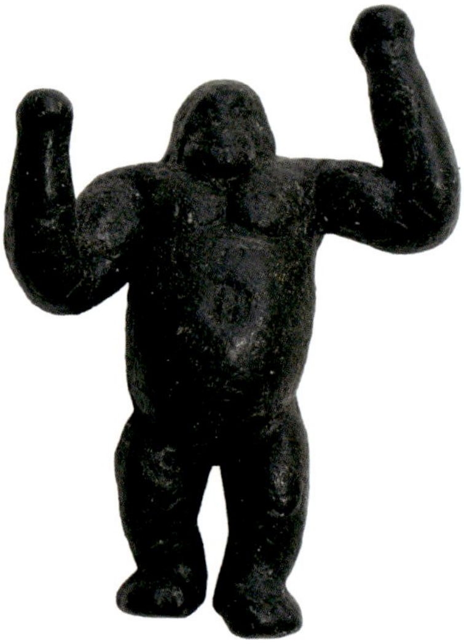

bananabottle, 2008, digital photograph portrait of marine debris.
kingkong, 2008, digital photograph portrait of marine debris.

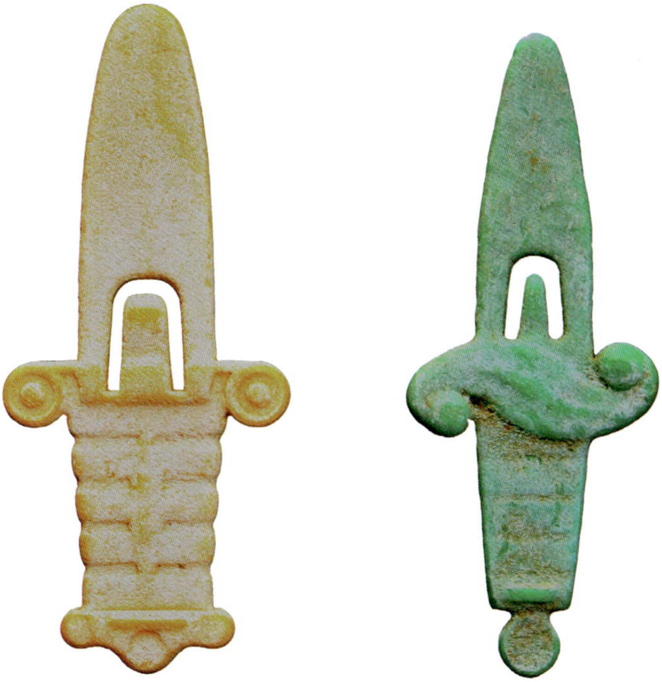

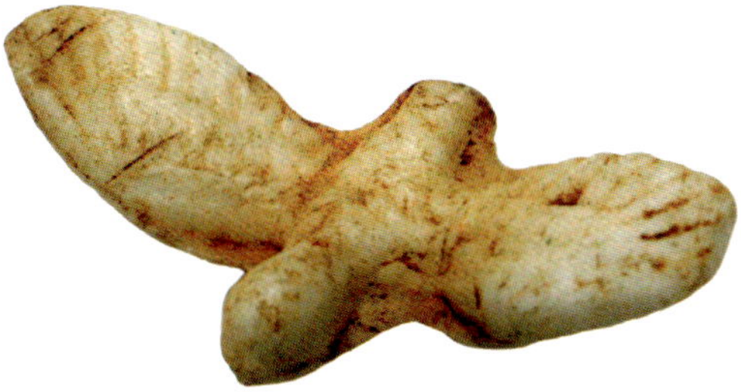

twoswords, 2008, digital photograph portrait of marine debris.
tinydove, 2008, digital photograph portrait of marine debris.

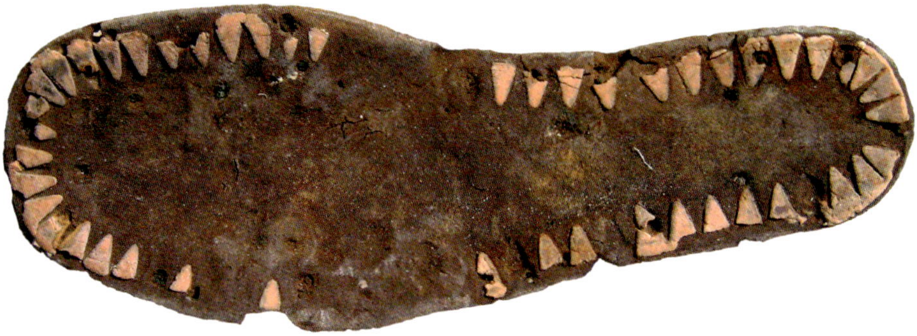

toothmouth, 2009, digital photograph portrait of marine debris.

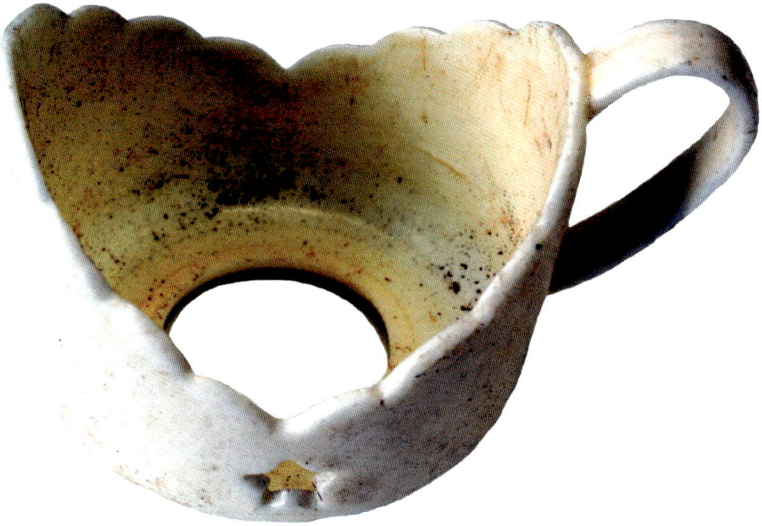

jawscup, 2006, digital photograph portrait of marine debris.

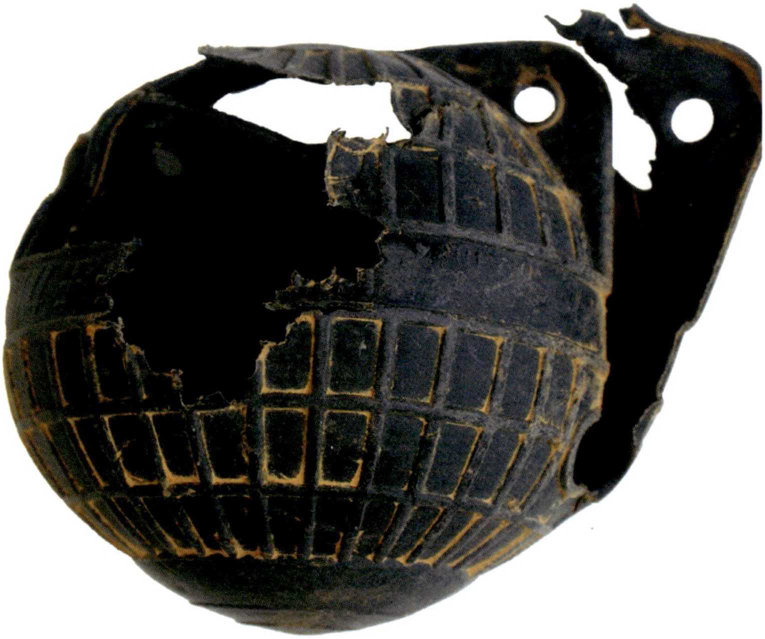

brokenworld, 2006, digital photograph portrait of marine debris.

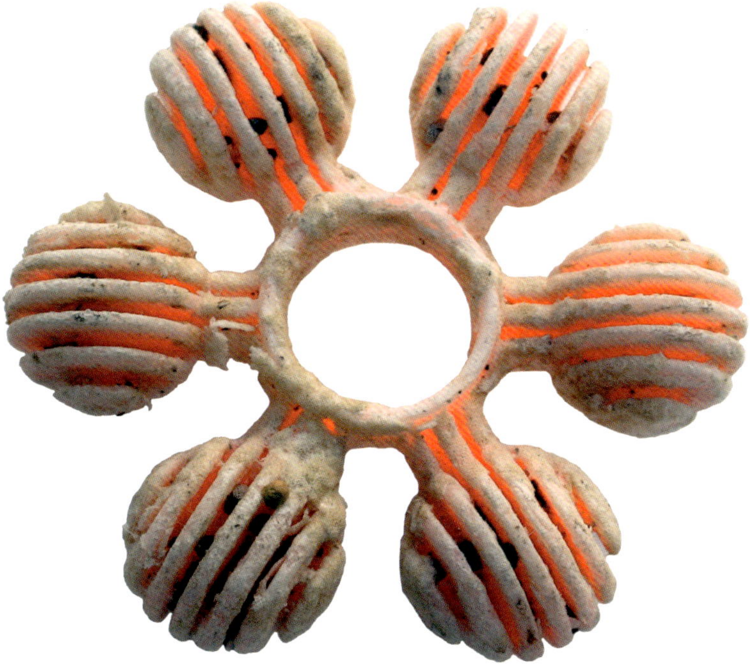

flowerballs, 2008, digital photograph portrait of marine debris.

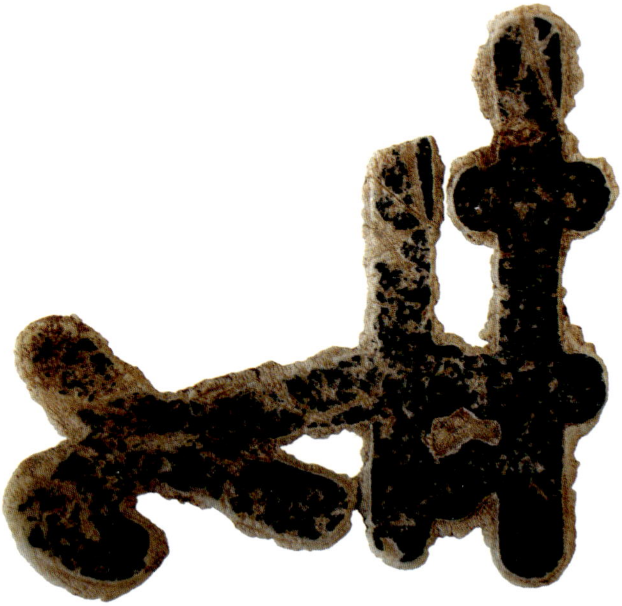

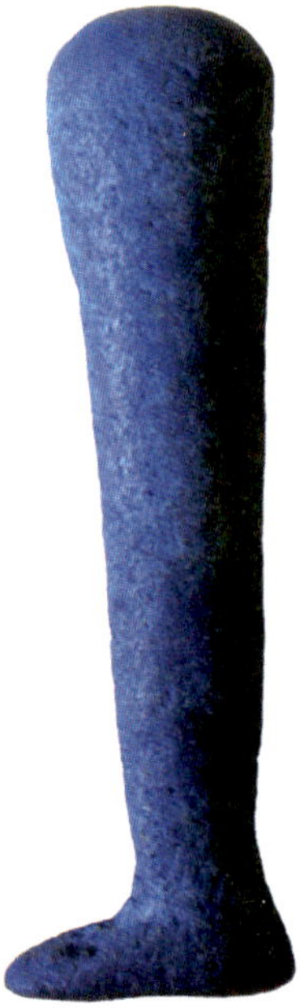

brokenletters, 2006, digital photograph portrait of marine debris.
blueleg, 2008, digital photograph portrait of marine debris.

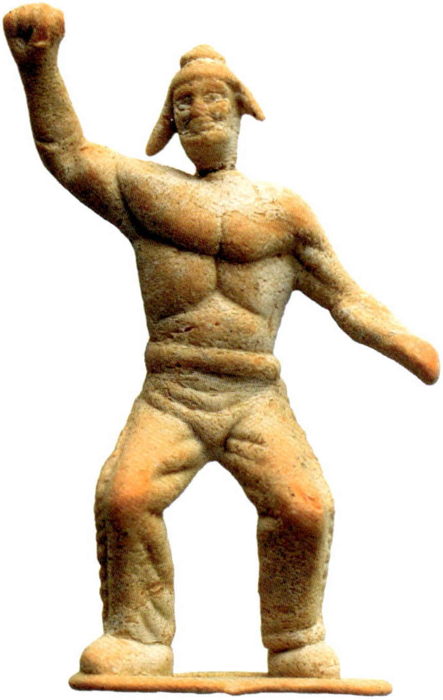

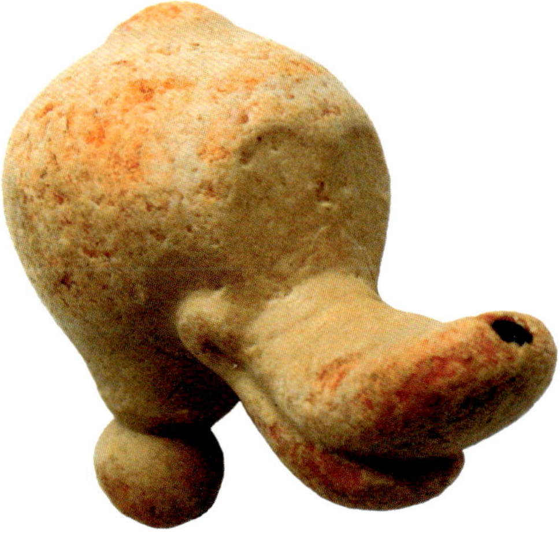

warriornomad, 2008, digital photograph portrait of marine debris.
plutohead, 2007, digital photograph portrait of marine debris.

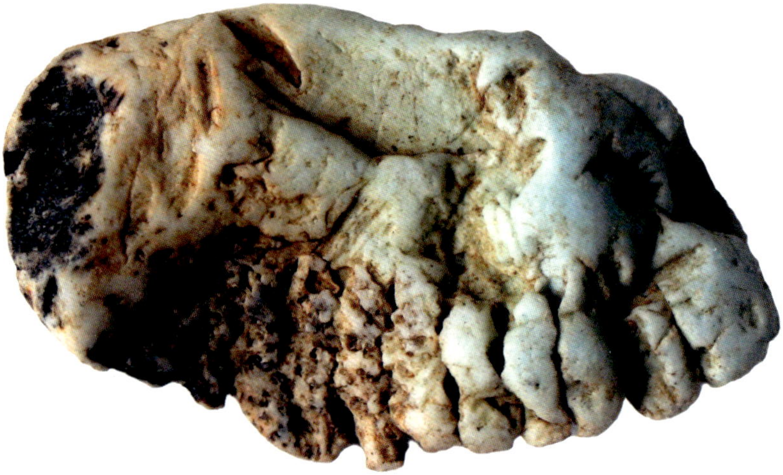

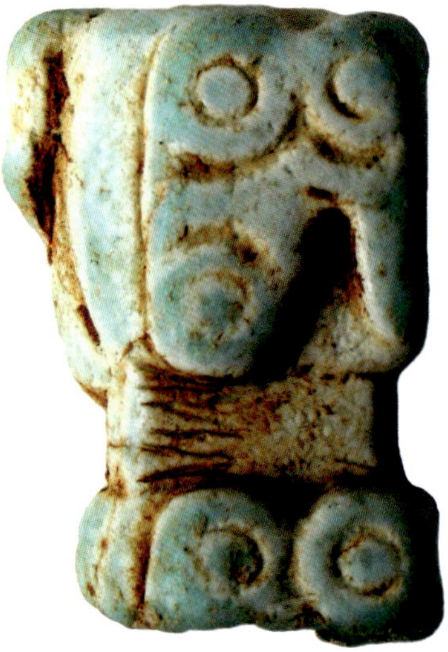

plasticjaw, 2006, digital photograph portrait of marine debris.
mayanbead, 2006, digital photograph portrait of marine debris.

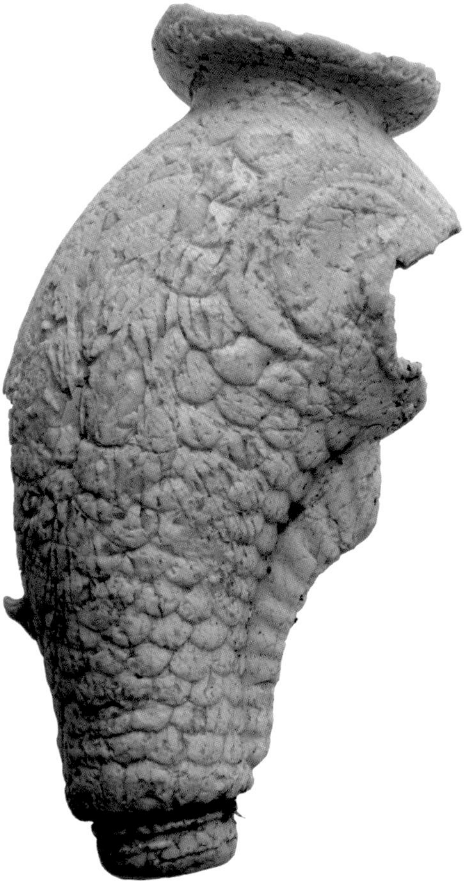

fishbottle, 2008, digital photograph portrait of marine debris.

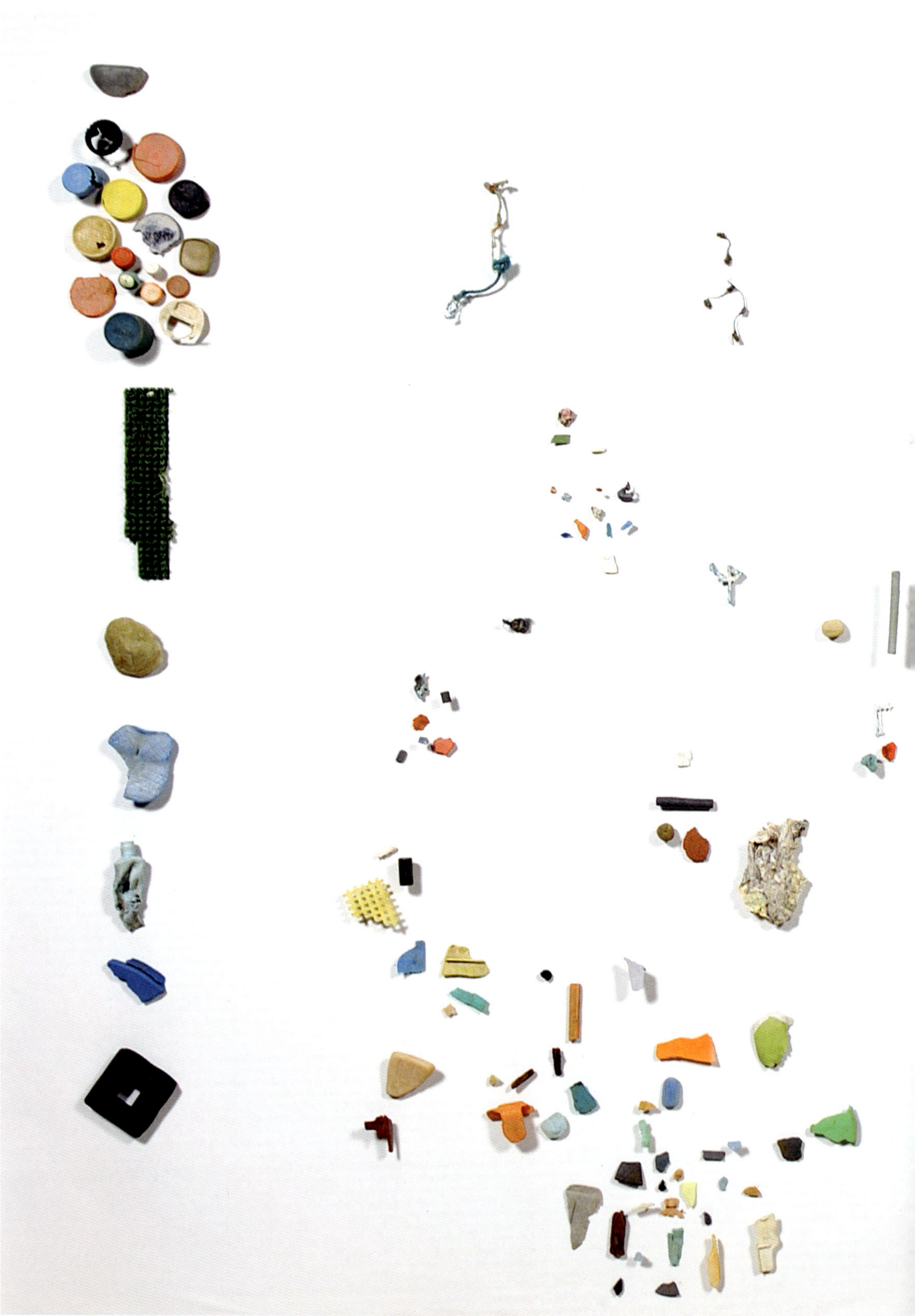

Defective Flow Chart, 2007, found plastic marine debris, silicone, steel pins, dimensions variable.

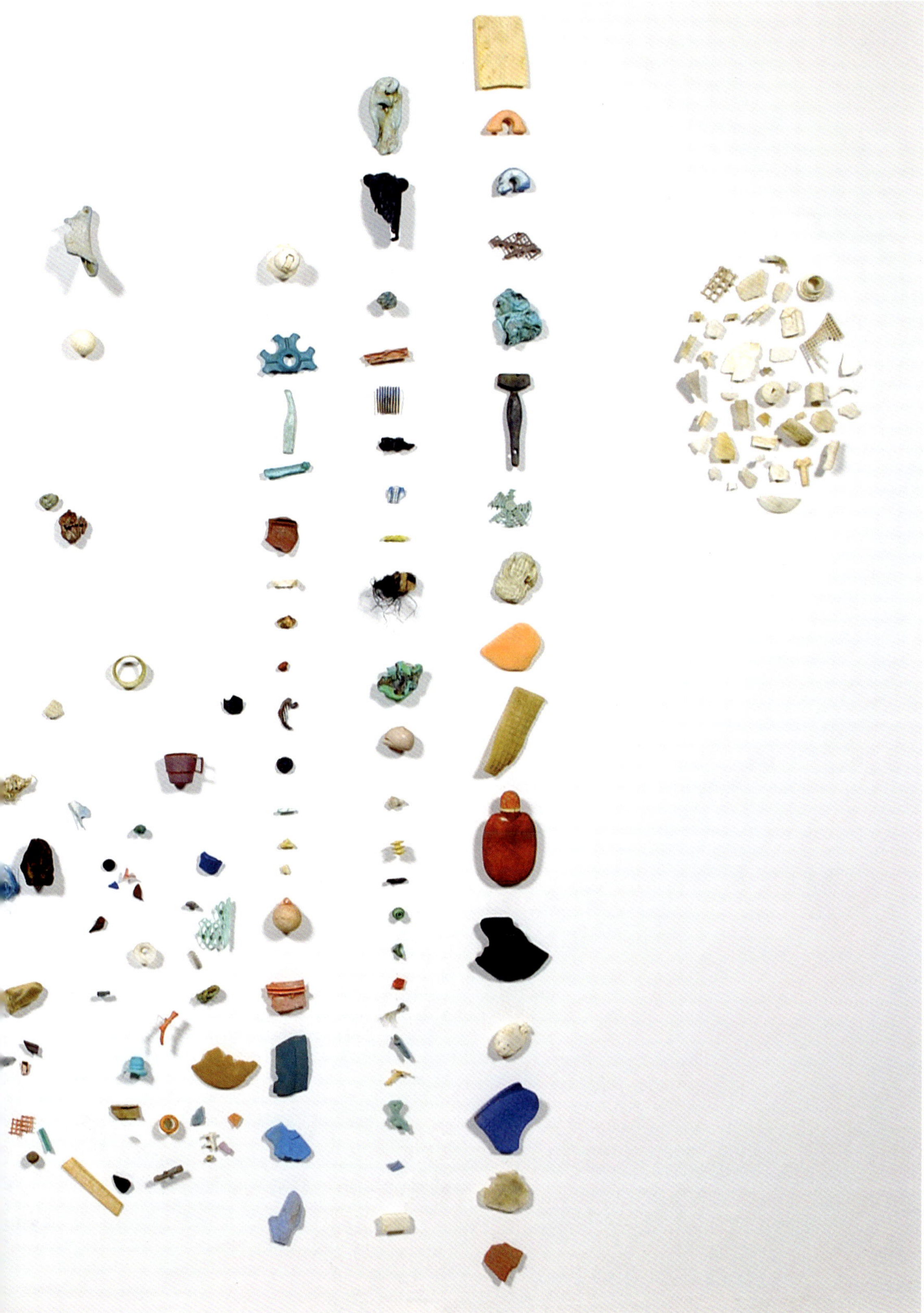

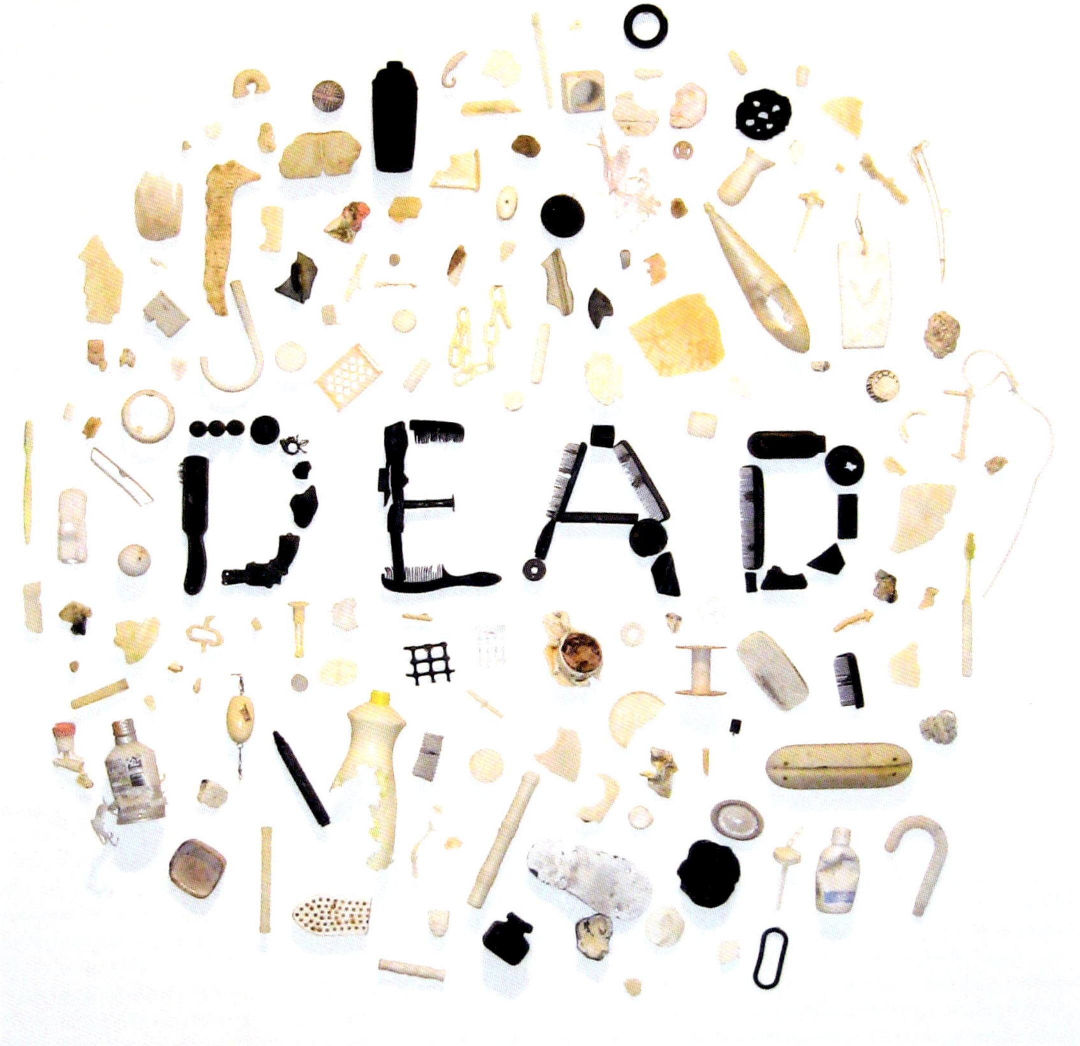

Eye Test Chart: Color Blindness (dead C red C), 2008, found plastic marine debris, silicone and steel pins, 2 parts, 48 in. diameter each.

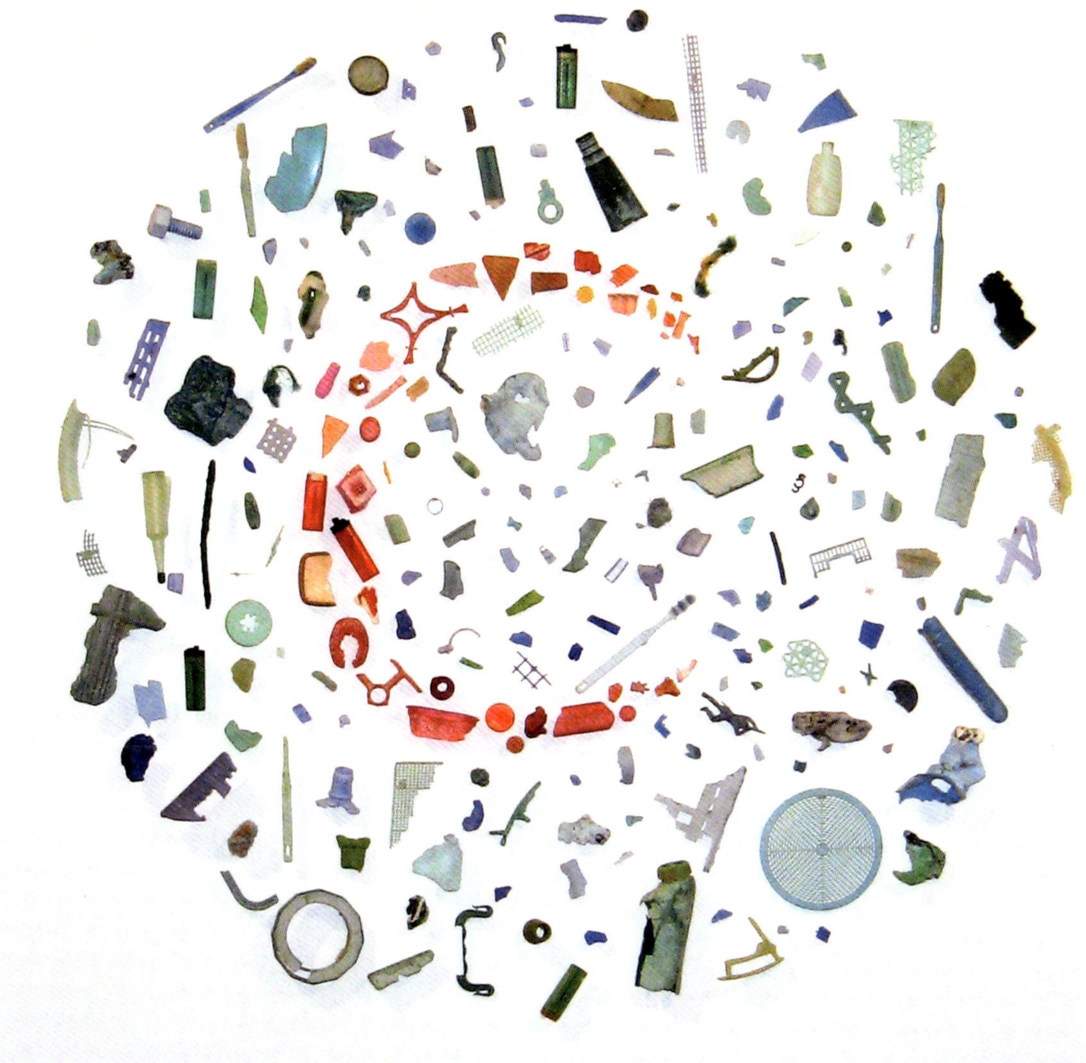

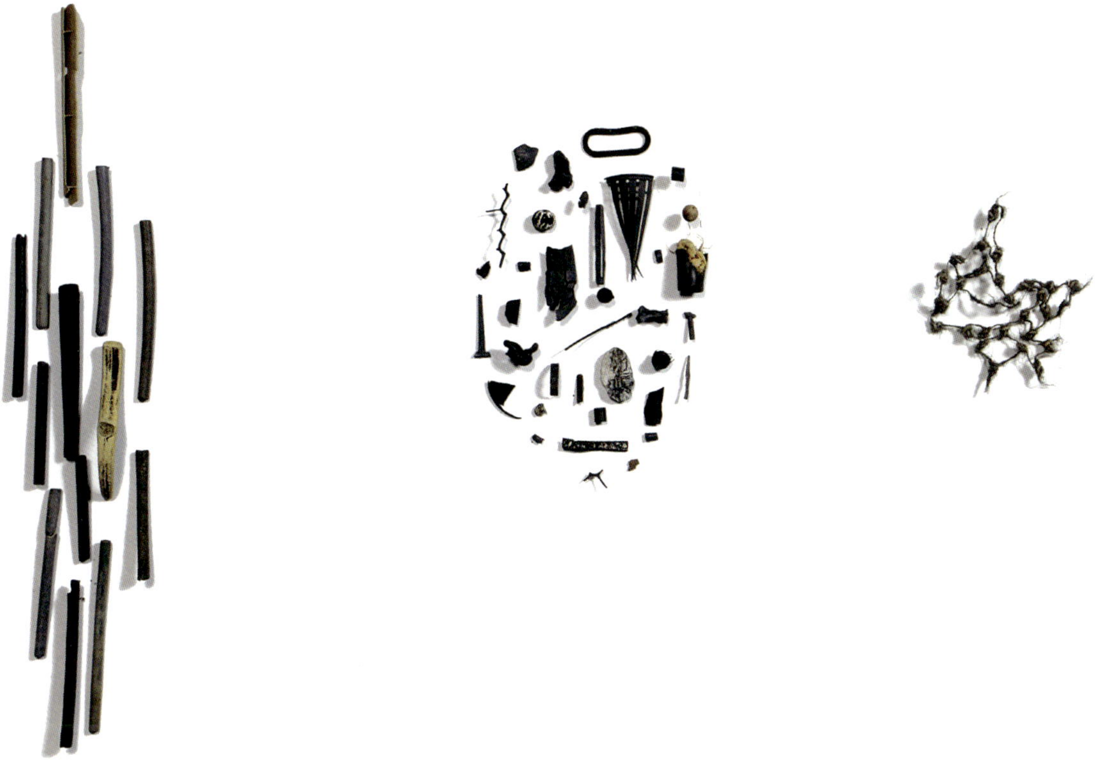

Use Value Vs. Exchange Value, 2006, found plastic marine debris,
South Point, Hawai'i, dimensions variable.

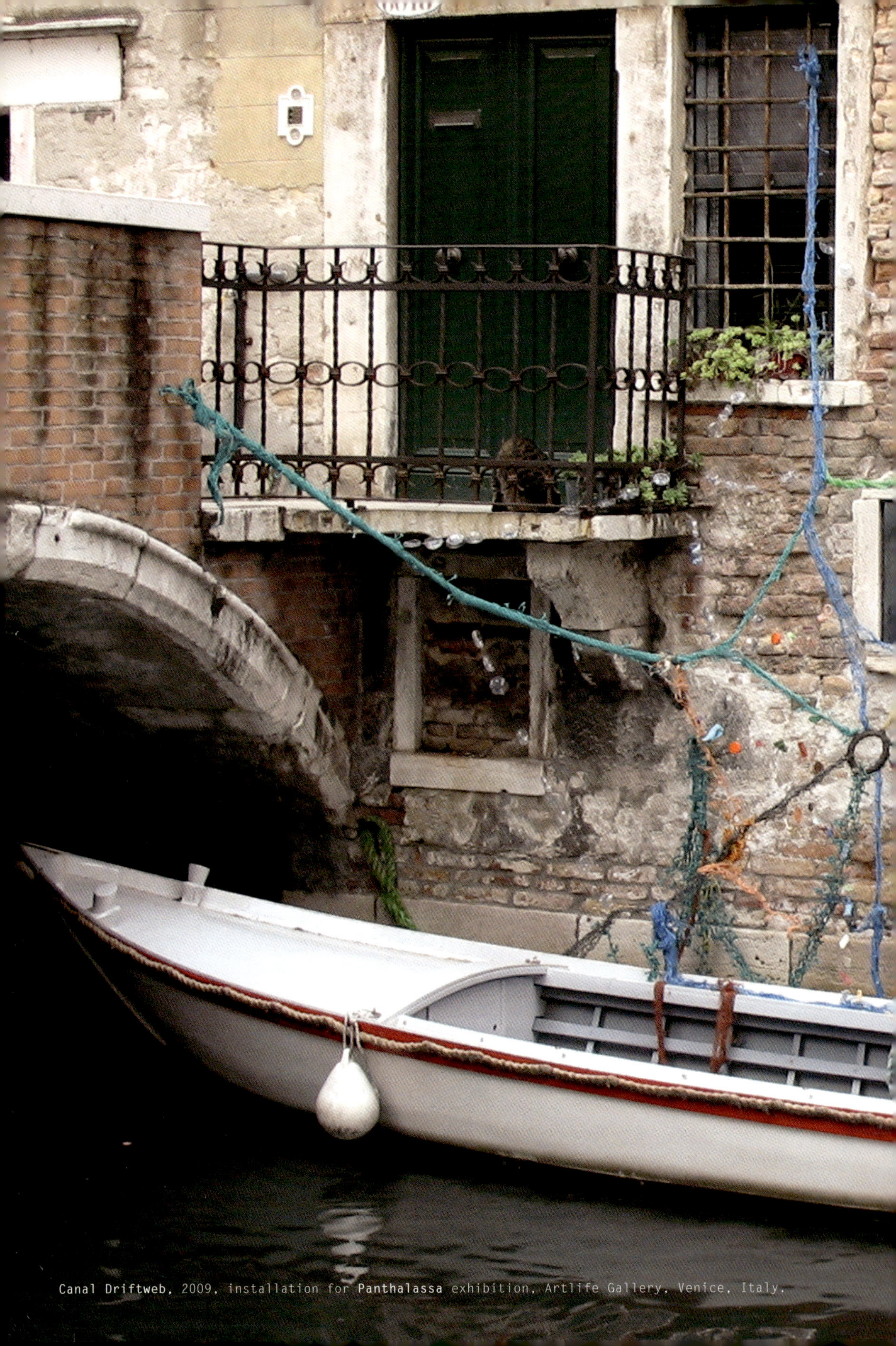

Canal Driftweb, 2009, installation for **Panthalassa** exhibition, Artlife Gallery, Venice, Italy.

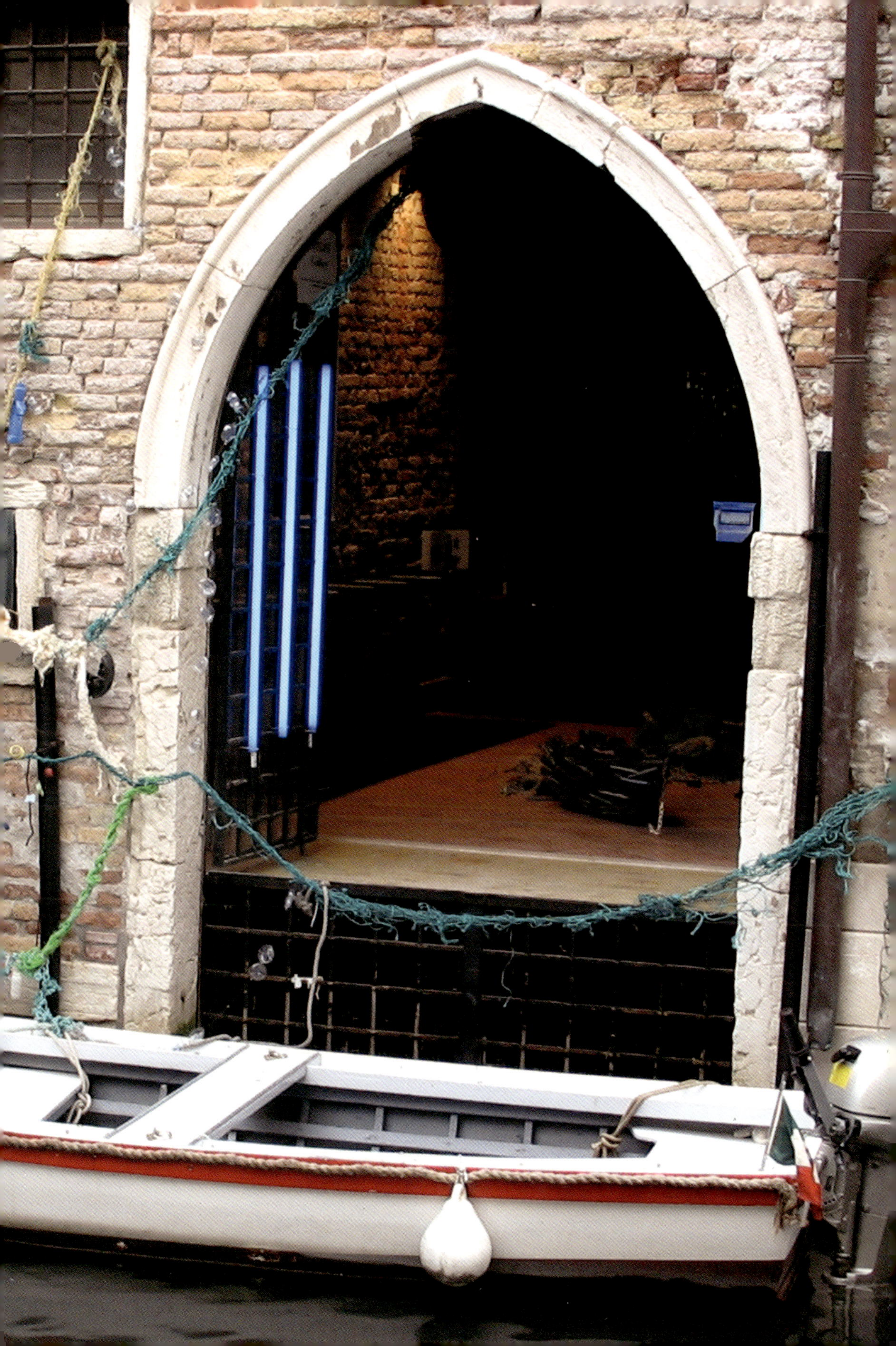

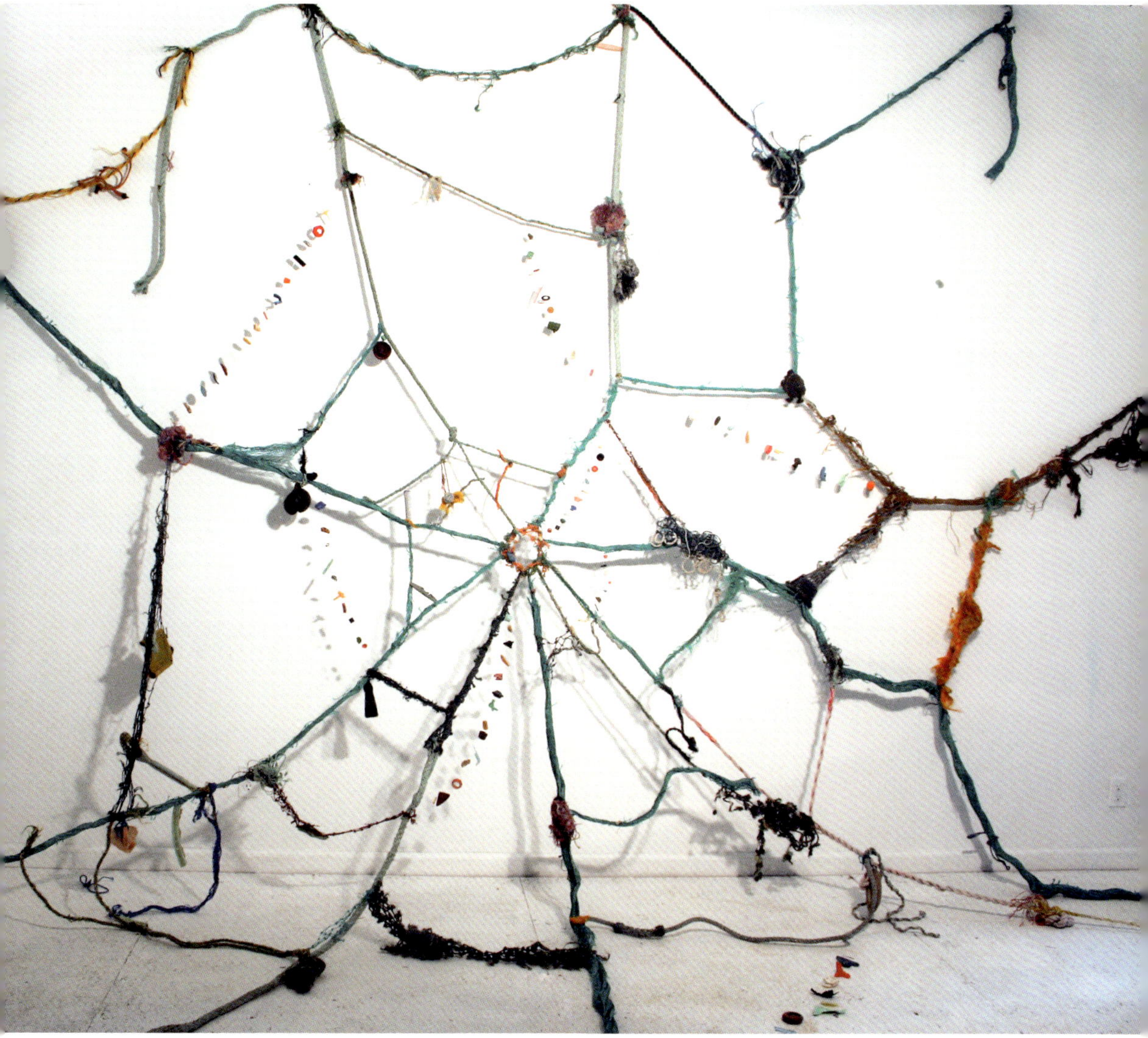

Driftweb I, 2007, found driftnet and plastic marine debris, dimensions variable.

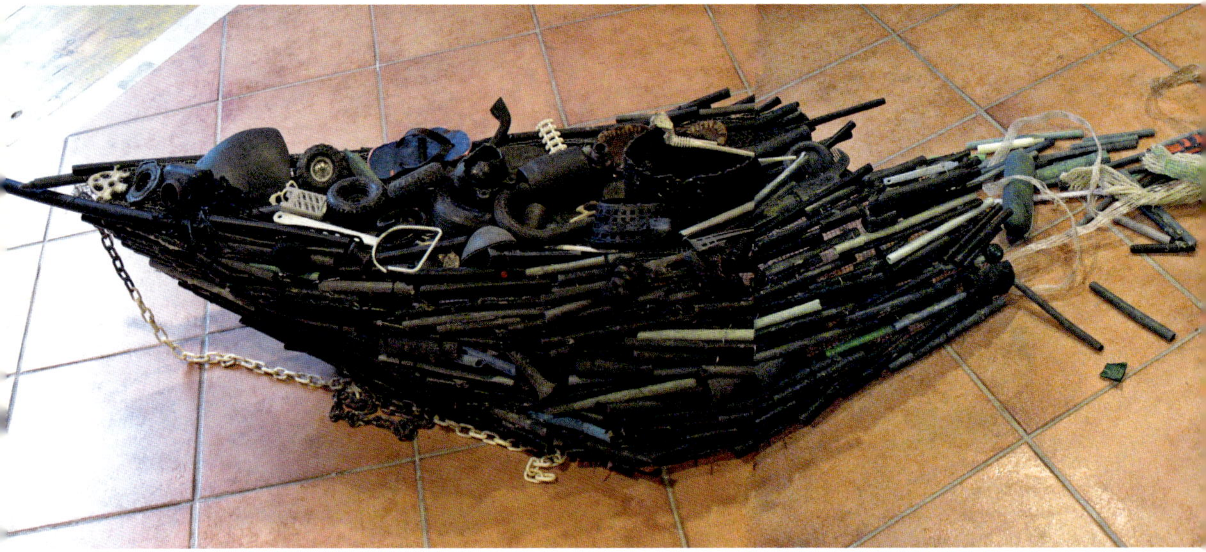

Shipwreck (Unintended Consequences), 2009, found plastic marine debris, silicone, steel wire and mesh, dimension variable.

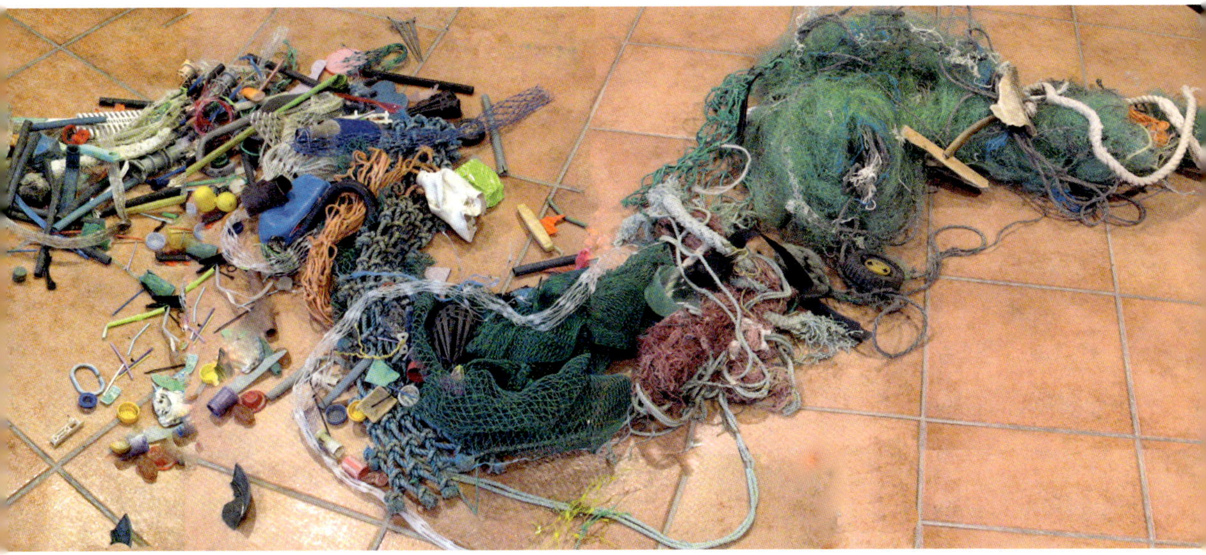

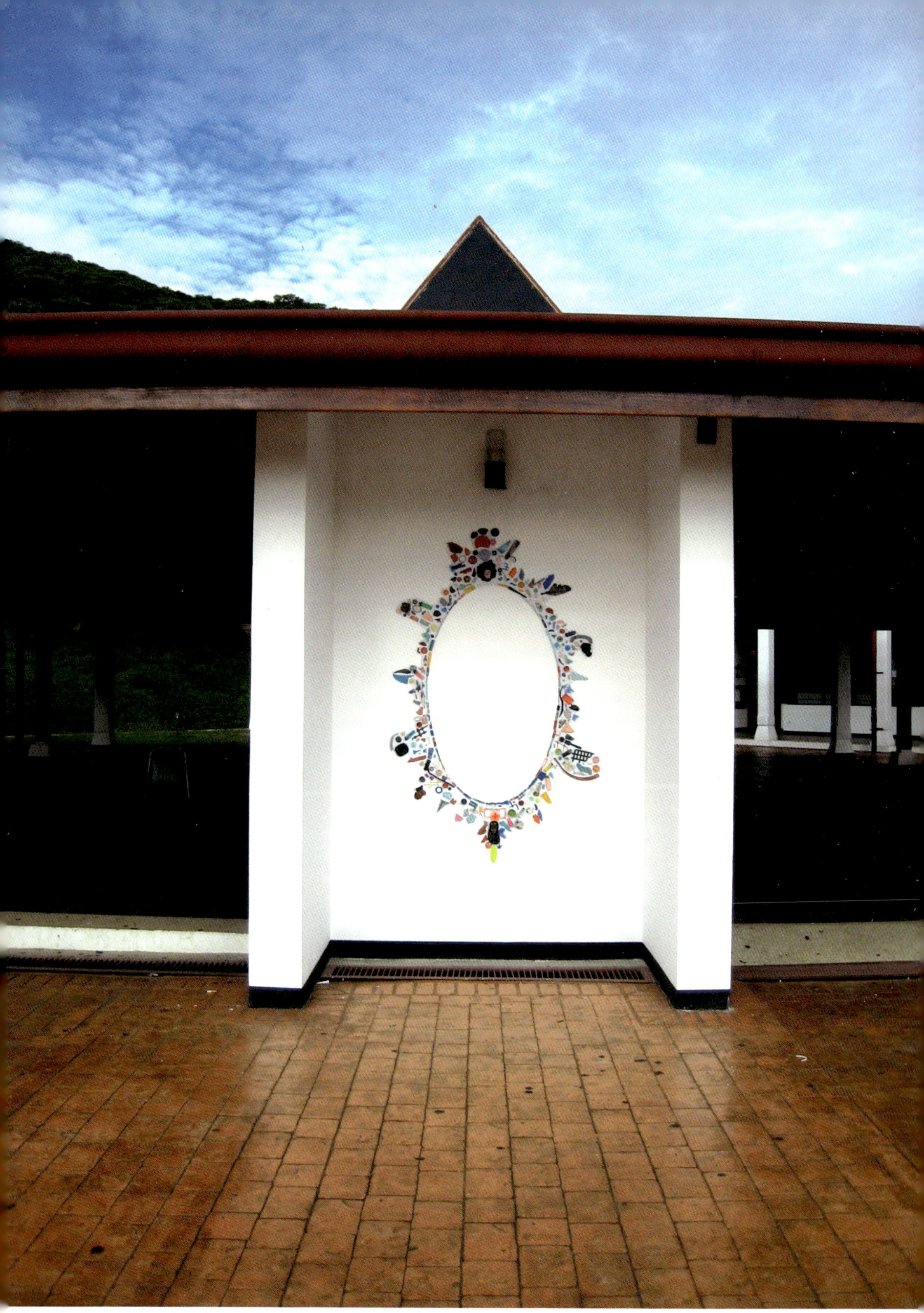

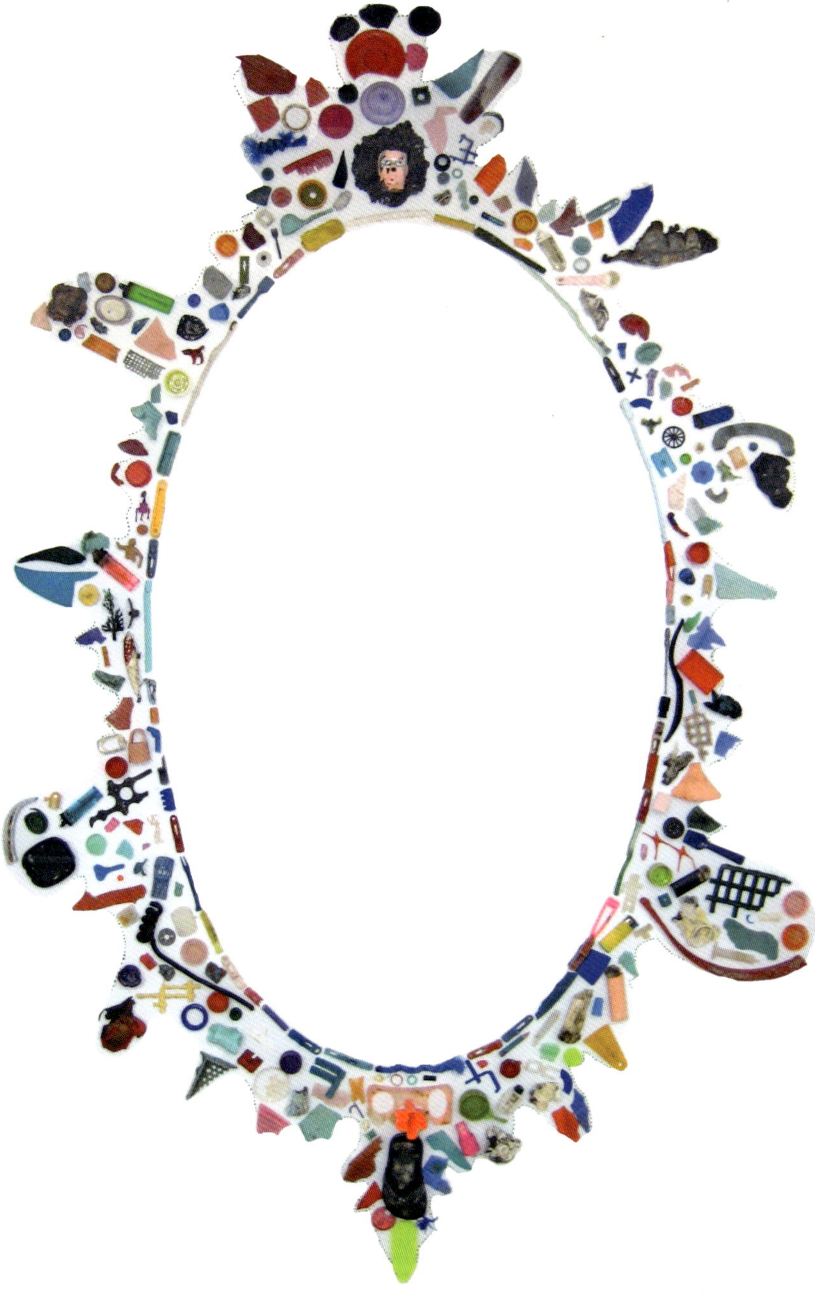

Human Mirror (For Sámara), 2009,
found plastic marine debris collected with volunteers from nearby coastal area, Playa Sámara.
Permanent public art installation, Universidad Nacional Sede De Chorotega, Nicoya, Costa Rica.

ABOUT THE CONTRIBUTORS

Carl Safina's *Eye of the Albatross* won the John Burroughs medal as best nature book of the year, and was chosen by the National Academies of Science, Medicine, and Engineering as the year's best book for communicating science. He is a MacArthur Fellow and President of Blue Ocean Institute, and author of other books about the changing ocean.

Dores Sacquegna is a critic, independent curator, and founder of the contemporary gallery Primopiano LivinGallery in Lecce, Italy (www.primopianogallery.com). She graduated from the Academy of Fine Arts in Lecce in 1993 and continued her studies in graphic art and printing at the International Association of Engravers in Rome. She represented Italy with two scholarships offered by the Ministry of Foreign Affairs at the Academy of Fine Arts in Luxembourg (1995) and the Academy of Art, Architecture, and Design in Prague (1997). Her curatorial work includes collaboration with international public and private entities such as: Saatchi & Saatchi (New York) and the Ray Of Light Foundation (New York) in support of the Harlem Art Project (New York, 2006); CCCB, the Center of Contemporary Culture of Barcelona, Spain, (2007/2008/2009); the Olympic Fine Arts Museum, Beijing, China (2008); and the Pinacoteca Gerger and Heraklion, Crete, Greece (2009). Among her most important curated exhibitions at the gallery in Lecce was the show *Antologica*, the national preview of the work of Hermann Nitsch (Vienna, 1938), the leading exponent of the Viennese Actionists, for which she worked in collaboration with the Fondazione Morra in Naples (2007).

Ron Broglio is Associate Professor of Literature and Culture at Georgia Gwinnett College and visiting scholar at the University of Waterloo. His research focuses on how philosophy and aesthetics can help us rethink the relationship between humans and the environment. He is author of *Technologies of the Picturesque* (Bucknell 2008) and *On the Surface: Thinking with Animals and Art* (Minnesota Press, forthcoming 2011). At University of Waterloo he is working with dairy farmers to create community art works around technological interventions on dairy farms.

ABOUT THE ARTIST

Pam Longobardi was born in 1958 in Glen Ridge, NJ; her parents, an ocean lifeguard and the Delaware state diving champion. She moved to Atlanta in 1970 and saw her neighborhood pond drained to build the high school she attended. Since then, she lived for varying time periods in Wyoming, Montana, California, and Tennessee, and worked as a firefighter and tree planter, a scientific illustrator and an aerial mapmaker, a waitress and a bartender, a collaborative printer and a color mixer. Her artwork involves painting, photography, and installation and addresses the psychological relationship of humans to the natural world.
She has shown her artwork across the US and in Finland, Slovakia, China, Japan, Italy, Spain, Belgium, and Poland.
She currently lives and works in Atlanta and is Professor of Art at Georgia State University.
Presently she drifts with her project to ocean shores from Hawai'i, Italy, Costa Rica, and elsewhere, intercepting and redirecting the plastic flow.

EDUCATION

1985
MFA, Master of Fine Arts, Montana State University, Bozeman, MT
1981
BFA, Bachelor of Fine Arts, University of Georgia, Athens, GA

SELECTED SOLO EXHIBITIONS

2009
Panthalassa, ARTLIFE Gallery Contemporary Art, Venice, Italy (September)
2008
Plastic Durations, NY Arts Beijing, Chaoyang District, Beijing, China (during the 2008 Olympics)
Drifters, Tinney Contemporary, Nashville, TN (October)
Drifters, Charlotte and Philip Hanes Gallery, Wake Forest University, Winston-Salem, NC (September)
2007
Drifters, Charleston Heights Art Center, Las Vegas, NV (November)
Drifters, Sandler Hudson Gallery, Atlanta, GA (January)
2006
Sky is Fallen, Sandler Hudson Gallery, rooftop installation, Atlanta, GA
2004
Worlds Within Worlds, Jacksonville Museum of Modern Art, Jacksonville, FL
Artificial Kingdoms, Sylvia Schmidt Contemporary Art, New Orleans, LA
2003
Drawing Voices: Encounter, Galerie Entropia, Wroclaw, Poland
2002
Pearl of the Third Mind, Gusto House Gallery/Free Space, Kobe, Japan
2000
world world, Lowe Gallery, Atlanta, GA
Visible/Invisible, Hartsfield International Airport Atrium, Atlanta, GA
Beyond the Frame, Knoxville Museum of Art, Knoxville, TN
1998
animal/beautiful, Lowe Gallery, Atlanta, GA, catalogue
1994
Appeals, Oaths, and Queries, Lowe Gallery, Los Angeles, CA
1993
Double/Split, Czech Cultural Center, Bratislava, Slovakia, installation
Double/Split (Desire), MUU ry, Gallery of New Media, Helsinki, Finland, installation
1992
Pam Longobardi, Kathryn Sermas Gallery, New York, NY

SELECTED GROUP EXHIBITIONS

2009

Evolutionary Drift: Pam Longobardi and Sue Johnson 98th Annual Exhibition of Contemporary Art, Maier Museum of Art, Lynchburg, VA, catalogue

2008

Selections from the Imagery Estate Winery Permanent Collection, Carnegie Art Museum, Pittsburg, PA

2007

POOL Art Fair/*Ocean View* at Miami Basel Art Fair, Cavalier Hotel, Miami, FL

POOL Art Fair/*Art Attack,* Chelsea Hotel, Chelsea Hotel, New York, NY

Broadthinking: Inaugural, Silent Space Gallery, Kingston, NY

2006

Birdspace, Tucson Art Museum, Tucson, AZ (January–March), curated by David Rubin, traveling for 2 years, with Ross Bleckner, Mark Dion, Walton Ford, Kiki Smith, Hunt Slonem, Petah Coyne, and others, catalogue

IV Biennial of Graphic Art, Francavilla Al Mare, Italy and Sant Carla de la Rapita, Spain

2005

New Orleans Triennial, New Orleans Museum of Art, New Orleans, LA

Imagining Escape, live flower installation, Ernest G. Welch Gallery, Atlanta, GA

2004

Breathing Space, Metaphor Contemporary Art, Brooklyn, NY

Adornment: Embellishment and Encroachment, Diboll Gallery, Loyola University, New Orleans, LA

Birdspace, Hudson River Museum, Hudson, NY; Norton Museum of Art, West Palm Beach, FL; Contemporary Art Center, New Orleans, LA; Tucson Art Museum, Tucson, AZ

2003

Skin: Contemporary Views of the Body, Jacksonville Museum of Modern Art, Jacksonville, FL

The Armory Show, Chelsea Piers, New York, NY

V. Rooms in Dialog, Zaal Scaldis Eiermarkt /Antwerp Tower Building, Antwerp, Belgium

2002

Art Chicago at Navy Pier, Chicago, IL

A Century of Progress: Twentieth Century Painting in Tennessee, Cheekwood Museum of Art, Nashville, TN

SELECTED AWARDS, HONORS, AND FELLOWSHIPS

2009

Artist in Residence, Bau Institute, New York; Otranto, Italy

2008

Artist in Residence, NY Arts Beijing, Beijing, China

2007

Artist Associate, Blue Ocean Institute, East Norwich, NY

2006

Artist Residency Fellowship, Red Cinder Creativity Center, Hawai'i

Outstanding Faculty Achievement of the Year Award, Georgia State University, Atlanta, GA

2005

Research Initiation Grant, College of Arts & Sciences, Georgia State University, Atlanta, GA

2003

Research Instrumentation Grant, College of Arts & Sciences, Georgia State University, Atlanta, GA

2000

Major Public Art commission, Atlanta Medical Examiner's Facility, Fulton Co. Arts Council

1999

Artist Residency Fellowship, Franz Masereel Center, Kasterlee, Belgium

Research Initiation Grant, College of Arts and Sciences, Georgia State University, Atlanta, GA

TABOO Project Grant, "Requiem" exhibition, Nexus Contemporary Art Center, Atlanta, GA

1998
Chancellor's Award for Research and Creative Achievement, University of Tennessee, Knoxville, TN
1996
Visual Artist Fellowship, Tennessee Arts Commission
1995
Major commission, MBL Life Assurance/1st Tennessee, Memphis, TN
1994
SAF/NEA Visual Artist Fellowship, painting

SELECTED BIBLIOGRAPHY OF REVIEWS AND CITATIONS

2009
Kjeseth-Johnson, Martha, "Evolutionary Drift," catalogue essay, Maier Museum of Art, Lynchburg, VA
La Nuova Venezia, La Repubblica, "Naufragio di plastica in Calle dei Miracoli,
http://ricerca.gelocal.it/nuovavenezia/archivio/nuovavenezia/2009/09/23/VGBPO_VGB02.html
Sacquegna, Dores, "Between Memory... and Chronicle...," catalogue essay, *Panthalassa* exhibition, Venice, Italy
Kaufman, Leslie, "Clearing the Coast," catalogue essay, *Panthalassa* exhibition, Venice, Italy
Platt, Ron, *New American Painting*, no. 82, Open Studios Press, Boston, MA, pp. 5, 112–115
Byrd, Cathy, "A (new) Genre Landscape," Sculpture, International Sculpture Center, May, pp. 72–73
2008
Patterson, Tom, "Ocean Debris as Subject and Material," *Winston-Salem Journal*, October 17
PBA.Org Programming, citation on website, http://www.pba.org/programming/programs/newgenre/2152/
Design Public, citation on weblog, http://blog.designpublic.com/2008/09/02/more-bottle-recycling-ideas/
Moriarity, Jim, OceansWavesBeaches, citation on blog, http://oceanswavesbeaches.blogspot.com/2008/03/pam-longobardi-at-first-art-imitates.html
Blue Ocean Institute, citation on website, http://www.blueocean.org/programs/art-poetry/art-view?id=2
NY ARTS Beijing, www.nyartsbeijing.cn/pfwebplus/ArtistResidency/RESIDENCE/lipDetailShow.aspx?Id=34
Visualized Whirled Peas, citation on weblog, http://river2sea72.wordpress.com/
2007
Fox, Catherine, "Terrible Beauty," *Atlanta Journal-Constitution*, February 4, p. 12
Keene, Jarret, "Plastic is Forever," *Las Vegas City Life*, November 22, p. 43
Morse, Marcia, "Nature vs. Structure," *Honolulu Weekly 'Hot Picks'*, September 5
Haute Nature, work cited, http://hautenature.blogspot.com/2007/12/drifters-salvaged-sea-net-art-by-pam.html
Moore, Alan W., "Basel Pesto," work cited, http://post.thing.net/node/1847
Brooklyn Museum Feminist Website, http://www.brooklynmuseum.org/community/blogosphere/feministbloggers/2007/08/
2006
Nugent, Bob, Forward by Donald Kuspit, *Imagery: Art for Wine*, Wine Appreciation Guild, pp. 140–141
Fox, Catherine, "Object Lessons," *Atlanta Journal-Constitution*, April 23, p. K 5
2005
Tuley, Laura, "Adornment: Embellishment and Encroachment," *Art Papers*, January–February, p. 45
2004
Perez-Brennan, T., "Creations Meld Science, Art," *Florida Times Union*, Jacksonville, July 9, pp. 15–16
Rubin, David, "Birdspace," exhibition catalogue, essay, pp. 21, 24, 26. Publ. by Pamela Auchincloss
Bookhardt, Eric, "Birdspace," review, *Art Papers*, July–August, pp. 44–45
2003
Rezerwuj Czas, "Dongoski w Entropi Jak Brzmi kreska," *City Magazine*, Wroclaw, Poland, July, p. 20
Co Jest Grane, "Zdarzenia z glosami,", *Gazeta Wyborcza Wroclaw*, Poland, June 27, p. 13
Strefa Miejska, "Drawing Voices," *Aktivist*, Wroclaw, Poland, no. 48, July, p. 17
McClellan, Marian, "Exploiting Nature's Finery," *New Orleans Art Review*, January–February, pp. 29–30

Yee, Ivette M., "In the Flesh," *The Times-Union*, Jacksonville, rev, May 2, p. 15
Kinghorn, George, "Skin: Contemporary Views of the Body," exhibition catalogue, essay, ill.
Carruthers, Valerie, "JMOMA: A Cultural Institution," Arbus, May–June, article, ill., pp. 52-61
2002
MacCash, Doug, "Off the Walls," *The Times-Picayune*, New Orleans, rev., ill., Dec 6
Bookhardt, Eric, "Worlds Within Worlds," *Gambit*, New Orleans, rev., ill. Dec 10
Duerr, Teri, ed., "Visual Feature," guest artist pages, *Kansai Scene*, Osaka, Japan, no. 26, June, pp. 21–23
2001
Fox, Catherine, "The Art of Afterward," *Atlanta Journal-Constitution*, December 30, p. L1, 10
Joyner, Heather, "Keys to Two Personal Kingdoms," *Metro Pulse Knoxville*, January, 4, p. 20
2000
Makrandi, Nandini, "Beyond the Frame: Pam Longobardi + Catherine McCarthy", catalogue, Knoxville Museum of Ar, Knoxville, TN
Krainak, Paul, "world/world," catalogue essay for exhibition, Lowe Gallery.
Cullum, Jerry, "The world as theme park," *Atlanta Journal-Constitution*, November 24, p. Q8
1999
Pessina, Maria, "Arte Crossover," *Radar no. 64*, El Universal/Caracas, Venezuela, March 3

SELECTED PUBLIC COLLECTIONS
Maier Museum of Art, Lynchburg, VA
Kilpatrick Stockton Attorneys, Atlanta, GA
Blue Ocean Institute, Cold Spring Harbor, NY
Corcoran Gallery of Art, Washington, DC
Knoxville Museum of Art, Knoxville, TN
Hyatt Regency International Hotel, Naples, FL
Arizona State University Art Museum, Tempe, AZ
Atlanta Hartsfield Airport, Atlanta, GA
Softblox Computing Technologies, Atlanta, GA
Tweed Art Museum, Duluth, MN
Saks Fifth Avenue, Atlanta, GA
Kennedy Art Museum, Athens, OH
MBL Life Assurance Corporation, Memphis, TN
Benziger Winery, Sonoma, CA
Hunter Museum of Art, Chattanooga, TN
Freeman-Hawkins Attorneys at Law, Atlanta, GA
Stockholders Systems, Atlanta, GA
Burroughs-Wellcome Pharmaceuticals, Raleigh, NC
Instituto de Estudios Norteamericanos, Barcelona, Spain
Miami Metropolitan Museum Art Center, Coral Gables, FL
Pratt Institute, New York, NY
Deloitte-Touche, Atlanta, GA
Knestrick Contractors, Inc., Nashville, TN
School of the Art Institute of Chicago, Chicago, IL
Clapsadle-Baugnet, Minneapolis, MN
Agnes Scott College, Atlanta, GA
Tennessee State Museum, Nashville, TN
Taller Galeria Fort, Barcelona, Spain
University of Tennessee, Knoxville, TN
Montana State University, Bozeman, MT
City of Atlanta, Art in Public Places, Atlanta, GA

∞

To find out more about Charta,
and to learn about our most recent publications, visit

www.chartaartbooks.it

Printed in December 2009
by Tipografia Rumor, Vicenza
for Edizioni Charta